Praise for *Imprints*

Filled with lessons of love and compassion, *Imprints* is a beautiful reminder of the life God calls us to live each day.

– Bob Goff, *New York Times* bestselling author of *Love Does* and *Everybody, Always*

Our lives are filled with choices. Every moment is an opportunity for us to bring light or darkness into the world. Patrick and Justin remind us how simple it is to choose light.

– Jeremy Cowart, artist and founder of The Purpose Hotel

It's impossible to engage with Patrick and Justin and not walk away inspired, curious, and ready to be the person you are meant to be in the world. *Imprints* is a moving reminder of finding strength in the small things—gestures of kindness and connection—and of how the culmination of these acts fills our own lives and communities with authentic purpose. A must-read reminder that it's the small steps of love that leave imprints along this path of life.

– Jessica Honegger, founder and co-CEO of Noonday Collection

Justin and Patrick are compelling forces for good. Their latest book, *Imprints*, is a must-read, one of those rare books that invites and guides you to step into brave new places with your one and only life. Their words will surely help you live the kind of life that demands an explanation.

– Steve Carter, pastor and author of *This Invitational Life*

If we knew that our actions and choices could be the bread crumbs that others could follow into a better life, would we live better? I think so. This book is the encouragement we need to live more intentionally, leaving a trail of hope and love to those around us.

– Dean Nelson, award-winning author and journalist

Imprints

Patrick Gray and
Justin Skeesuck

From the Award-Winning
Authors of *I'll Push You*

Imprints

The Evidence
Our Lives
Leave Behind

Tyndale House Publishers, Inc.
Carol Stream, Illinois

Visit Tyndale online at www.tyndale.com.

Visit Compassion online at www.compassion.com.

Visit Patrick and Justin online at www.pushinc.us.

TYNDALE and Tyndale's quill logo are registered trademarks of Tyndale House Publishers, Inc.

Compassion and Compassion International® are registered trademarks of Compassion International,® Inc.

Imprints: The Evidence Our Lives Leave Behind

Designed by Justin Skeesuck

Published in association with the Christopher Ferebee Agency. www.christopherferebee .com.

For information about special discounts for bulk purchases, please contact Tyndale House Publishers at csresponse@tyndale.com, or call 1-800-323-9400.

ISBN 978-1-4964-4189-8

Printed in the United States of America

25	24	23	22	21	20	19
7	6	5	4	3	2	1

To our wives—thank you for the constant love and support
as we pursue the next adventure, whatever it may be.
To our children—you have taught us so much. Our prayer for
each of you is that others will know love because of who you are.

Contents

Foreword

by Seth Haines, author of *Coming Clean*

ANN CURTIS WAS A SLIGHT WOMAN who stood somewhere near average height, if you included her silver beehive hairdo. She was a woman of few words, at least as far as I knew, but still, her life spoke plenty. It was well known that Mrs. Curtis took the morning shift in our church prayer room. In fact, it was rumored Mrs. Curtis took two morning shifts and would sometimes cover a third on account of the fact that said hour was claimed by a traveling salesman whose morning calls and morning prayers were sometimes at odds.

Mrs. Curtis lived across the street from the prayer room, a convenience for the slow-going woman, because she spent the majority of her day there. Her husband had passed some years before (how many I couldn't say), and instead of becoming some kind of assisted-living hermitess, she committed to spend what days she had left serving the church in prayer.

Every morning Mrs. Curtis walked to the church, sometimes stopping by the bakery afterwards to grab a loaf of bread, a pastry, or a pint of milk. She did a great deal of walking, I remember, and I think this was because she had some kind of difficulty driving. In my young estimation, the trouble with driving was brought on by neither old age nor senility; instead, it was the sort of trouble brought on by a hairdo that didn't much cooperate with being mashed against the ceiling liner of her old Buick. So Mrs. Curtis walked just about everywhere, lips moving all the while in prayer.

When I was fifteen, our church youth group held one of those Don't-Have-Sex-Till-You're-Married retreats made popular by the Evangelical 1990s. At the closing ceremony of the retreat, the pastor invited us to sign pledge cards vowing to wait till marriage to taste the sweet fruits of monogamous marital bliss. I signed my card, walked to the front of the church, and placed it on the platform. The pastor then invited the congregants to make their own pledge.

"Come to the front and take a card," he said. "Pledge to pray for the person whose name you draw until that person is married."

Even then, I questioned whether such a commitment was feasible, but as fate, fortune, and the Holy Ghost would have it, Mrs. Curtis drew my name. She never told me that she had come into possession of my pledge card, though. She never broached the subject of purity or lust with me, which is good, because the awkwardness quotient of any such conversation would have been rivaled only by the time Sister Sarto had the "sex talk" with my class of sixth-grade boys in Catholic school. Instead, if Mrs. Curtis ever exchanged words with me at all (a fact I do not recall all these years later), it wasn't much more than simple pleasantries.

I went on to college, and as young men tend to do, tried my best to leave my hometown behind. I didn't think much about my old church or the faithful men and women who'd attended for so many years, Mrs. Curtis included. And so, seven years and two children into marriage, you can imagine my surprise when someone called to tell me Mrs. Curtis had passed away.

"I'm sorry. But why are you calling to tell me?" I asked.

"I want you to know," the calling minister said, "that Mrs. Curtis kept your pledge card in her Bible till the day she died. I happen to know that she never missed a day of praying for you, even after you were married."

For over a decade, she'd prayed for me. For over a decade, those prayers had been a sort of guide, even if I hadn't known it. For over a decade, she'd given time to me. And as I stood gape-mouthed on the other end of the phone, I knew her prayers had left their mark. Ann Curtis had left her imprint on my life.

Imprints—each of us will leave them along the way. Some will use their time, talents, resources, and words in more selfish ways, leaving negative and lasting imprints on their families, friends, and communities. Others, like Mrs. Curtis for example, will leave a different sort of imprint, an imprint that speaks of the reality of God's Kingdom. In this book, Patrick and Justin don't just analyze, examine, and teach us how to leave a Kingdom imprint (though they do that in spades), they pay homage to the men and women who've left Kingdom imprints on their own lives. Through their own experiences, they give us a cast of characters—coworkers, friends, and a cast of otherwise serendipitous acquaintances—who've lived lives of intention, lives that have made an impact. You might not recognize their names, and you couldn't pick them out of the crowd, but the people in this book are the great saints of this world. They are people who've dedicated themselves to knowing God and making him known.

As you read these pages, take note. Discover how to live in a way that's present to the world around you, that's mindful of the mark you'll leave. Press into that understanding and let it shape the time you have left here on earth. After all, though your money, success, and accolades may fade, your imprints carry on. And on. And on.

Introduction

WE LIVE IN A BROKEN WORLD. Every time we turn on the television or peruse a news feed, pain, suffering, and negativity lead the headlines. Not a week goes by where we don't hear about riots, mass murders, starvation, or abuse—so many people in so much need. If you're like us, this often feels overwhelming. With so much hurt at every turn, it's easy to feel defeated—to feel as if nothing we might say or do could even begin to make a difference.

If we want the world to heal and hope to rise, we must understand that the little things we do every day have great significance.

Then we hear the story of a man or woman who has started a nonprofit equipping people in developing countries with food, water, homes, and educational resources, or a team of individuals raising millions to combat homelessness through shelters, counseling services, and job placement programs.

Our hearts swell with hope—someone out there is actually making a difference, fighting against the darkness. But there is a lingering feeling that what *we* do still doesn't matter, because *we* aren't feeding starving children or building homes for the homeless. This lie can subtly work its way into our hearts and minds—and if we aren't careful, the lie becomes truth—we believe we aren't enough, and as a result, we stop doing the things that matter.

If we want the world to heal and hope to rise, we must understand that the little things we do every day have great significance. No matter how large a person's platform or how world-changing their organization, a legacy isn't built on grand acts. It is the culmination of all the little things we do—this is how we fulfill our purpose. The legacy we pass on to future generations is who we are when we think no one is watching, how we live our lives in the day-to-day: the way we treat a waitress, the times we acknowledge servicemen and servicewomen for their contribution and sacrifice, the moments we look a grocery clerk in the eyes and call her by name. These little things in everyday situations carry weight; they are significant—because no act of love goes unnoticed and no deed of compassion is futile. There are a million moments in each of our lives where we have the opportunity to bring joy or pain, light or darkness, heaven or hell to others

> **Who we are on a day-to-day basis is the greatest testament to what we believe.**

through the words we say and how we say them; through the things we do and how we do them. Each one of us has significance, because each one of us has the power to bring love and compassion to the lives of every person we meet.

Yes, the world needs nonprofits that build freshwater wells in African villages or equip underserved communities with medical resources. But living in a manner where we actively seek opportunities to love in simple yet profound ways is just as, if not more, important. Every day is filled with moments in which we can positively impact our friends, families, significant others, children, and strangers—because every single act leaves a mark on the lives of those around us, for good or ill. Every decision, every word leaves an imprint on others, but we often fail to notice these imprints because we don't appreciate the influence we have on our world.

Who we are on a day-to-day basis is the greatest testament to what we believe. The way we treat others and the intentions behind our actions leave impressions on those we encounter. These marks are the evidence our lives leave behind.

Every one of us has remarkable power and influence. Understanding this is the first step toward making this world a better place.

Part One
We're All Guides

God may not guide us in an obvious way because he wants us to make decisions based on faith and character.

– Dallas Willard

LIFE IS A JOURNEY filled with millions of decisions. Some are as simple as what we eat for lunch or when we choose to go to bed. Others, though, have lasting consequences, implications not only for our lives but also for the lives of others. The tone of voice we use when frustrated with a child, the way we respond to a stranger who cuts us off in traffic, the words we choose when talking about people who think or act differently than we do, the way we treat those who can do nothing for us—these behaviors affect not only the people they're directed toward, but also those who observe them.

Every day, we are guiding others down a path. We can influence their faith and help shape their character, or we can take them down a path of pain and destruction. Is our path filled with love, grace, mercy, and forgiveness? Or is our road marked by hate, insecurity, self-doubt, and fear?

Someone is always watching. Someone is always listening. Someone is always following.

Whether we like it or not, we're all guides. Where are you taking those who choose to follow you?

Your Life Is a Compass

1

History is not everything, but it is a starting point. History is a clock that people use to tell their political and cultural time of day. It is a compass they use to find themselves on the map of human geography. It tells them where they are, but more importantly, what they must be.

– John Henrik Clarke

FOR THOUSANDS OF YEARS, sailors have used the heavens to guide their journeys through unknown waters, discovering new or forgotten places, or cultures previously unknown. And just as grand adventures across the sea were successfully navigated by bright stars in distant space, men and women were able to find their way home from their grand adventures because of reference points in the sky. Some ancient cultures believed the heavens were filled with gods or celestial beings that provided safe passage, guidance, and wisdom. Many prayed to the stars or the entities these stars represented to help them find their way.

The most significant celestial body used in ancient navigation is the constellation Ursa Minor. Over millennia, the axis of earth's rotation came to point at what we refer to as the North Star (part of Ursa Minor), and it became the focal point for maritime navigation rather than the entire constellation. This ball of fire in distant space has gone by many names: Polaris, Alpha Ursae Minoris, *scip-steorra* ("ship-star" in Old English), Dhruva (Hindu for "fixed" or "immovable"). But no matter the name used or the ocean sailed, every sailor looked to this star (or group of stars) for orientation. Every map drawn and navigation chart created was done with this star's position in the sky in mind. Why? Because it identifies true north. It is a reliable guide.

But using a star as a reference point works only at night. And often clouds blocked man's view of the sky, storms filled with wind and rain obscured both horizon and the heavens, and crews found themselves off course because true north wasn't visible. Distractions or dangers residing much closer than a distant star compromised many a journey through the open ocean. But for thousands of years, stars in distant space were the best the world had to offer.

> **In life we need direction, something to point us toward the good we want to do and the people we want to be.**

More than two thousand years ago, the Chinese developed an invention that would revolutionize navigation, on and off the water. The first compass, made of lodestone, was crafted in the Han Dynasty between 300 and 200 BC. Due to the earth's magnetic field, this naturally magnetized iron ore is attracted to the North Pole, making it possible for travelers to identify true north even when the North Star isn't visible.

It turns out we can learn a lot from a compass.

In life we need direction, something to point us toward the good we want to do and the people we want to be. We need help navigating dark times or simply dealing with changes that catch us off guard. Sometimes we don't know we need a course correction, but our lives are desperate for it. For many, faith provides this direction; it is our true north—the thoughts, ideologies, and philosophies that inform our decisions and guide our actions. But faith is something we can't touch. While we experience it in various ways, we can't see it, and often it feels out of reach, like the distant North Star. And just like this star, our faith can easily be hidden, clouded by distractions, and our reference point is lost from view.

These distractions come in many forms: trauma, addictions, selfish behaviors, financial struggles, unexpected deaths, disease, divorce. The list of things that derail us is long because we have a million different things vying for our attention. The storms of life bring wind, rain, and dark clouds that can completely obscure our faith. It is in these times that we must rely on things much closer to us to keep our hearts and minds focused on what's important. We must find a compass that can help point us in the right direction, so when the clouds part, we don't find ourselves lost at sea.

Each person we know has the capacity to guide us: gently, and sometimes firmly, shifting our focus, turning us toward the things that matter. Their life experiences and what they have chosen to do with those experiences can be the compass we need to show us true north, clarifying the path we need to be traveling. Each person's history can help us understand where we are, but more importantly, their story can help us understand what we must be. They guide us in being better employees, parents, siblings, or children. They increase our capacity for love and grace as we strive to be the best friend, mentor, or spouse we can be. Our lives are filled with compasses waiting to be used at every turn. We find these people in our churches, workplaces, book groups, friendships, families, kids, and even strangers.

Our lives are filled with compasses waiting to be used at every turn.

College was a challenging time for me (Justin). I had left my family and my home in small-town Ontario, Oregon, for a much busier lifestyle in San Diego; my best friend, Patrick, was going to school a thousand miles away in Idaho; and a progressive neuromuscular disease was slowly stealing life from my body. A car accident had triggered the disease when I was fifteen, and throughout my college years, it crept its way deeper into the tissues of my legs. I had to give up tennis and running because my strength and balance were fading. Eventually I had to use braces to keep me from falling to the ground when walking.

Despite the support these braces offered, walking to classes became too much for me on the hilly campus of Point Loma Nazarene College, so I was forced to drive to many of them. As I navigated college life, questions about my purpose in this world and doubts about my future often crept to the surface of my mind. *How long will I be able to walk? Will I ever find someone who will love me despite my failing body? Will this disease eventually take my life?* Each year of college brought many struggles, primarily due to my disease.

But my four years pursuing higher education were also exciting. I got to stretch my wings as I sought independence, experienced new restaurants, explored new subjects, discovered new relationships, and learned from some amazing people.

My parents and many friends have had a remarkable influence on me, but during this time in my life, one man stands out—not because he was a better mentor, but because he possessed something that, though I didn't know it at the time, I would one day desperately need.

One sunny San Diego day during my sophomore year at Point Loma, I drove to class, parked my car in a handicap spot, and began walking to my nearby classroom. On my way there, a stranger approached me. With a warm smile and firm handshake, he introduced himself. Jim Johnson said he'd stopped me because he saw the braces that supported my lower legs; I assumed his curiosity had gotten the best of him, like so many other people on campus. Not a week went by where someone didn't ask, "What's wrong with your legs?" I had gotten used to the curiosity and did my best not to get annoyed. But in our conversation, I learned that Jim was a professor of Disability Studies and Psychology at Point Loma. He had taken an interest in what I might be dealing with as a disabled student. Throughout the remainder of my college career, we frequently encountered one another on campus, and every time, Jim stopped me and asked how I was doing. He sought to learn how my disease was impacting me physically and emotionally, and he always encouraged me.

Questions about my purpose in this world and doubts about my future often crept to the surface of my mind. *How long will I be able to walk? Will I ever find someone who will love me despite my failing body? Will this disease eventually take my life?*

I never took a class from Jim, but our conversations always stuck with me. However, it wasn't what we talked about that carried the most weight. Jim always had time for me. It felt like the world stopped during our interactions. Every discussion started with a hug, an embrace that told me I mattered. Jim's genuine interest in me as a person, what I was doing with my life, and where I was going, always took me by surprise. He frequently told me to see past my disability, to not let it define me. While I hadn't necessarily let my limitations define me, I certainly hadn't recognized how much I could do or what I could be in the face of my disease. Jim saw the potential in every person he met, and he saw purpose in me, even when I didn't see it in myself. And I saw something in him, something that I didn't have but wanted.

After graduation, Jim and I saw each other less frequently. But one day he invited my soon-to-be wife, Kirstin, and me to sit down with one of his disability-focused classes. Sitting in front of thirty or so young men and women, I was a little nervous. The topic was the impact of disability on relationships. I don't remember the details of the class session, but I do remember the love and respect Jim showed to each student—the same love and respect he always showed me. Jim was so proactive in cultivating relationships, so kind and compassionate; this was what I had seen in him several years earlier that I wanted to possess.

But life got busy. I got married, my wife and I had children, and my disease progressed. Honestly, life didn't just get busy—it got hard. Being a father and a husband in a wheelchair took me down some dark roads, and I needed someone I could look to for guidance. I needed a compass to point me in the right direction so when the clouds parted, I wouldn't be lost. I needed Jim. Though he wasn't disabled, and we had very different life experiences, Jim's ability to build love, compassion, and empathy with all he met drew me to him in a powerful way.

When I called Jim to tell him I needed someone to help me navigate this life I was facing and asked if he would be my mentor, he said yes without hesitation.

Over the next several years, Jim and I spent hours in conversations discussing life, death, faith, and love. And through them all, I was reminded of how the love and compassion Jim showed me was the same love and compassion I wanted to show others. His life wasn't perfect—he had his own demons—but in spite of the pain he battled, he chose to love others and not focus on his own darkness. It's not that he ignored it, but sharing in the pain of others, and sharing his pain with them, made everyone's struggles easier to bear. I needed to do the same thing.

Though I have long since moved from San Diego, I still come

back to those conversations and the wisdom Jim shared so many years ago. His conviction that I had purpose is something I have leaned on time and time again through recent years. Now, I live life from a power chair, unable to use my arms or legs. I am dependent upon my wife, Patrick, and others for care. They feed me, bathe me, help me go to the bathroom. Life is a struggle; there is always a darkness lurking nearby. But because of Jim, and others like him, I have something to point me in the right direction, even when I can't see where I need to go.

Jim's life has been a compass for me in many ways. The random encounters on campus carried just as much weight as the hours of mentoring over coffee. My relationship with Jim has evolved as we have grown closer. But that first moment, when he approached me as a complete stranger, looked me in the eyes, and treated me with so much compassion, is one I return to often. It is a powerful reminder that my life is a compass for others, whether I like it or not. Even a brief encounter has the potential to change someone, to offer hope, or to develop into a deeper connection. While I'm not always proud of where I am taking those that follow me, knowing that my decisions and actions can have an impact on someone else, just as Jim's decisions and actions have influenced me, is a powerful motivator to live in such a way that I am proud of where I am taking others.

———

We all have a history, events that shape who and what we are. And when others turn to us for help, our histories can help shape who and what they are: a young woman using her abusive childhood to help others in similar situations, a man's interest in cars leading to an after-school program to keep teens off the street, a college student volunteering at the local homeless shelter because she knows what it's like to be alone and scared. Our lives are filled with a host of opportunities to provide direction to others. The beliefs and behaviors we exhibit are a guide for others when they have lost sight of their true north or need to be pointed in a direction they never knew existed.

This can be a terrifying realization, because the idea that we are constantly influencing others means we have the power to lead them off course. Highly magnetized objects or locations can compromise the integrity of a compass. Many ships have gone down because a compass was distracted by other forces and wasn't pointing the right direction. In the same way, when we allow ourselves to be influenced by selfish desires, anger, or deception, we can easily lead people to disaster. We can be the broken compass that points others to dangers waiting just below the surface of the water: the "cool" neighbor who gets a kid to try drugs for the first time or the friend who starts a rumor about someone who has slighted them. Damage is so easy to cause. Casting a negative influence on others is simple when we are driven by selfish desires or anger-filled motivations, or are deceptive in our intentions. When have you led others off course, when have you been the cause of pain or darkness for someone else? If we are honest with ourselves, we have all been there. We have caused pain; our behaviors have fueled addictions; our selfish desires have led us to put our needs above our friends, spouses, and children. Every one of us has been a broken compass at some point in time. We all have given others bad information or pointed them down a path of pain and suffering. And still people follow.

So what are we to do? How can we ensure that we are worth

> **The beliefs and behaviors we exhibit are a guide for others when they have lost sight of their true north or need to be pointed in a direction they never knew existed.**

following? How do we know our history will be one that points others to where they should go and to what they should be? We don't have all the answers. But we do know this—if we lead with compassion and love, if our actions are fueled by a desire to ease suffering and pain, our compass will point others to a place where that same love and compassion abound.

And that is a direction always worth following.

Adventures Are Everywhere

2

We live in a wonderful world that is full of beauty and charm and adventure. There is no end to the adventures that we can have if only we seek them with our eyes open.

– Jawaharlal Nehru

WE HUMANS LOVE the gratification and excitement we experience through the adventures we pursue. And while adventure is something most people seek, we experience it in a variety of activities and to varying degrees. Some of us look for the extreme as we climb mountains, dive into underwater caves, backpack through remote mountains, or bike across entire countries. Others travel far and wide, embracing new cultures, taking in exotic landscapes, and exploring forgotten cities. But most of us find adventure in things a little tamer, like camping trips, family vacations to theme parks, day hikes through nearby foothills, or the day-to-day gratification of successes at work, the joys of parenting, and connection in relationships.

No matter where or how we seek them, life is full of adventures big and small. Some we plan, like annual vacations, while others find us when friends say, "I've got an idea." Regardless of their origin, the grand adventures tend to overshadow the ones we experience in our everyday lives. But it's these adventures in the routine of life that are the most significant, the ones that shape and mold us today into the people we will be tomorrow. Unfortunately, many of us fail to recognize the beauty sitting right in front of us because we are so focused on the next big thing, or we allow the mundane to camouflage the brilliance that is our life.

———

My wife, Donna, and I (Patrick) met during our freshman orientation at Northwest Nazarene College in Nampa, Idaho. We fell hard and fast. Since we were both broke, we spent most of our dates in one of our respective dorms playing cards and eating cheap pizza.

Unfortunately, many of us fail to recognize the beauty sitting right in front of us because we are so focused on the next big thing, or we allow the mundane to camouflage the brilliance that is our life.

We tied the knot on June 28, 1997, three weeks after college graduation. Our first three months together were spent living in Bothell, Washington, but the rain and traffic of the greater Seattle area drove us crazy, so we pulled out a map of the United States, grabbed a dime, closed our eyes, and tossed the coin in the air, saying we would move wherever it landed. A few weeks later we packed up our tiny apartment and moved south to Vancouver.

When we relocated, we had only one car and what felt like no money. Donna needed our car to drive to her substitute teaching jobs at nearby schools, but I also needed a vehicle to get to my new job working on the docks in nearby Portland, Oregon. So we took out the last $1,000 we had in our savings account and bought the only car we could afford: a white 1985 Honda Civic, complete with tiger-striped interior and a bullet hole in the passenger side door.

A year later, Donna got a teaching job in Meridian, Idaho, where I drove that car for four more years. More than once the broken gas gauge got the best of me, and Donna would have to come to my rescue.

During those first several years of our life together, we often struggled to pay the bills, had many a date that consisted of the same cheap pizza from college and a few hours at the dollar theater, and we worked second jobs to pay off school debt and to save for things we wanted or needed. Because of the extra income, we were able to take all kinds of trips—road trips to the coast, weekends in a cabin in the mountains, flights to see friends and family far and wide. In 2001 we saved everything we could and spent nearly four weeks in Europe with Justin and Kirstin. We traveled to France, Switzerland, Germany, Austria, and Belgium with nothing but the packs on our backs. The freedom we experienced was incredible as we explored new cultures, sampled decadent foods, and met so many beautiful people.

From 1997 to 2005 we were kid free as I tried to figure out what I wanted to be when I grew up. While Donna pursued a career in elementary education, I spent those eight years working in road construction, loading freight on docks, researching for Fish and Game, helping manage a sporting goods store, teaching high school, and eventually landing on a career in nursing. But throughout my career confusion, we always knew we wanted a family.

Early on in our relationship, Donna had told me she felt she was supposed to adopt a child. Soon after the birth of our oldest child, Cambria, in 2005, we started the adoption process for a child from China.

We had it in our heads that we would have three kids spaced two years apart. Because the adoption process was supposed to take a year to eighteen months, we had it all planned out—Cambria, a child from China, and then one more. Five years, a miscarriage, and another child later, we finally got the call that our little girl was waiting for us to bring her home—and we needed her to complete our family. Cambria was five, and our son, Joshua, was a year and a half when we left them in the capable hands of my parents, boarded a plane, and embarked on a journey that would take us halfway around the world to meet our youngest daughter, Olivia, then seven months old.

Twenty plus hours flying to Hong Kong, another few to Guangzhou, China, and we were finally there. Some details are a blur, but I'll never forget the day we met our little girl. A caregiver brought our daughter to us, and Donna took her in her arms, saying, "Hello, little Olivia." She reached up, grabbed a strand of my wife's hair, and smiled. Our family was finally complete.

Throughout our seventeen days in China, we dealt with paperwork, visited Olivia's orphanage, met with government officials, and loved on our girl.

When we arrived at the airport in Boise, Idaho, our family was waiting for us. Cambria and Josh rushed to us as we came into view, both bursting into tears. The transition back home had begun. It would take some time for our two oldest to get used to their new sister, and even longer for Olivia to adjust to her new life. Until then she had spent every day of her short life in an orphanage, and now she was in a world where nothing was familiar.

Before we adopted Olivia, I had worked at an area hospital in a job I loved, but with a new child on the way, money was going to be tight. So I took a new job—one that offered a higher salary and better benefits, but it was the night shift. I was often not at my best. Lack of sleep and living on a different schedule from my wife and three little ones meant I was missing a lot of little things happening right in front of me.

Not long after Olivia joined our family, I changed jobs again, which meant more money, more responsibility, and longer hours. I had jumped out of the frying pan and into the fire. Feeling constantly drained, I lived for the weekend, holidays, or vacation. Way too busy and longing for the big adventures in life, I was missing out on the little ones.

In my new role, I worked directly with a number of surgeons. One in particular took me under his wing. Howard was patient and wise and understood work-life balance better than most. A couple of years into the job, my responsibilities and workload increased. It was too much work for one person to handle. One day Howard sat down in my office and said, "I'm concerned about you. Life is full of adventures, and I think you're working so hard you're missing out on some of them. Life is a marathon, not a sprint. You need to slow down." It would take two more years of working in that role and a five-hundred-mile journey through Spain before I would truly understand what he was saying. (Sometimes I'm a slow learner.)

A lot has happened since Howard said those words to me, but they have hung with me. I don't always heed them well, but when I do, they make me slow down and think about the adventures I value most. I wouldn't trade the trips with Donna in our early years of marriage, our weeks in Europe with dear friends, the seventeen days in China, or five hundred miles across Spain for anything. There are so many other big adventures filled with memories. But these aren't the events that matter most to me.

When I slow down and focus on what has shaped me, the adventures that I hold most dear, they're the simple things—sharing a pizza and playing cards with Donna, walking together holding hands, a tiger-striped Honda Civic. Witnessing the birth of my children, building forts in the playroom. Nerf wars with Josh, watching Olivia dress up and dance her way into a room, the brightness that enters Cambria's face when I hold it in my hands and tell her I love her. These are the adventures that matter most.

I don't know how many moments like these I have missed out on because I've been distracted by the "big things"—pursuing success, working long hours to provide financially while failing to provide what is really needed. But I do know these moments are more important than anything else in this world. The little adventures are what make life worth living. It's these small yet defining moments that make the big adventures we share so beautiful.

In June of 2018, my family and I spent a week on the Oregon coast in a town called Waldport—just the five of us and our new dog, Ranger. We dug in the sand, played in the surf, built forts on the beach, and rested in each other's company. When we experience things together, when we take the time to see the wonders all around us through the eyes of others—through the eyes of our spouse, our children, friends, family—we get to step into the greatest adventure we can know. In moments like these we begin to understand who other people are, and only then can we truly appreciate the beauty God has placed in the people we are lucky enough to love.

———

Humanity has a knack for getting distracted from the important things in life. We find ways to busy ourselves with things that don't really matter, or we fill the voids in our hearts—often voids we've created through losing touch with who we are meant to be—with poor decisions and risky behaviors. Chalk it up to boredom, complacency, or whatever you like; we have a remarkable capacity to make decisions that can wreck our marriages, destroy our friendships, or compromise our relationships with our children because we are pursuing the wrong adventures.

But there is a flip side to that coin. We can fill our lives and our hearts with beauty. When we slow down and open our eyes to the little adventures unfolding right before us in the everyday moments, we get to participate in one of the grandest adventures ever known—relationships with others. One of the most important facets of a healthy relationship is shared adventure. When we slow down and see life through the eyes of those we claim to love, we draw closer to them because we begin to understand who they are, what they want to be, and where they want the world to take them.

When we slow down and embrace the small things with our kids, our spouse, our families, and our friends, those little adventures make the big ones so much better.

> When we slow down and open our eyes to the little adventures unfolding right before us in the everyday moments, we get to participate in one of the grandest adventures ever known—relationships with others.

Read books with your kids. Lie in bed next to them and dream up tomorrow's possibilities. Take a walk with your spouse and breathe in the fresh air as you take in your partner's beauty. Sit with a friend over coffee or wine and listen to their dreams and ambitions.

Pursue the little adventures so when you get to share the big ones they can be everything you hope for and more. Not because of the adventure itself, but because of the relationships those adventures represent.

Colorful Language

3

The soul becomes dyed with the color of its thoughts.

– Marcus Aurelius

OUR WORDS HAVE REMARKABLE POWER. We can use them to create or destroy, build up or tear down, heal or hurt. Our lives slowly become identified by the words we use and the way we use them, and others see us as the things we create with our tongues.

When we speak joy, people see us as joy-filled. When we voice love, people see us as loving. And when we use words filled with kindness, patience, caring, and grace, the rooms we walk into are changed—attitudes shift, negativity subsides, and a peace that wasn't present before creeps into our conversations and relationships.

But when we frequently choose angry words, we are known as angry people. When we speak with hate, others see us as hateful. And when our conversations give life to contempt, breathe out negativity, and inflict pain, we bring that same contempt, negativity, and pain into the lives of all we encounter.

Unfortunately, we often underestimate the power we possess

and fail to steward our words the way we should. Sometimes it helps to look at our impact on the world through a fresh lens.

Children can be full of wisdom, often unknowingly. They just tell it like it is, when they have the freedom to do so.

One of the young ones in our lives recently said, "We are like a box of crayons. The words we use color the world around us."

Out of the mouths of babes often rise incredible life lessons—that is, if we take the time to listen and make an effort to understand.

The words we use color the world around us.

This concept of viewing words as colors caught our attention. What if instead of viewing them as a box of crayons, we thought of our words as a collection of paints? A palette of many colors, one for every emotion we possess and each action we take?

———

So much planning and preparation go into having a baby. Sometimes surprises catch us off guard, but nine months is usually enough time to get a few things in order.

We purchase cribs and changing tables. Rocking chairs stand at the ready. We pick out curtains to provide accent colors. And we adorn the walls with soft pinks, bright blues, beautiful greens, or warm yellows. We decorate bedrooms and playrooms with colors that reflect the joy the wee ones bring into our lives . . . that is, until they don't. Because parenting is hard. It's difficult to find joy in tantrums or sleepless nights. And for every step taken and successful bathroom excursion accomplished, there is a couch marked with ink or a pair of dress shoes filled with water.

> "We are like a box of crayons. The words we use color the world around us."

As children grow, sporting events, sleepovers, and birthday parties come in equal parts stress and fun. Teenagers test the waters like they did when they were three, but with more confidence and less forethought.

From the day they're born, children bring every possible emotion to the table—joy and pain, happiness and sadness, laughter and tears. And while we relish the highs of parenting, perhaps even more defining for our children is how we deal with the lows.

A child's bedroom is meant to be a safe haven, somewhere he or she can retreat from the world, a place of rest. But it only takes a few words of anger and frustration to taint the sanctity of a child's room with rage and fear. If we think of our words as brushstrokes of different colors, this is like stomping into a room of soft pinks or bright blues and splashing the walls with angry reds and dark grays.

> **Just a few short, anger-filled sentences can repaint every room in the house.**

Just a few short, anger-filled sentences can repaint every room in the house. Heated arguments and judgment cast upon others over the dinner table can make the dining room a place our children dread, walls covered in black. The living room can become a place our sons and daughters avoid because of dismissive comments, hateful rhetoric, and condescending statements.

Countless scholars, theologians, and peacemakers have explored the power that rests in our words. And every religion agrees on their ability to create and destroy.

Our words can be so hard to tame. Even if we never cross the line of abuse, we can still cause lasting damage. Though the tongue has no bones, it is strong enough to break hearts and scar souls.

An angry father can easily treat his young children as less than. Soon words of frustration and anger outweigh the times he tells them he loves them, and over time, the home becomes a place they don't want to be.

A mother can reach her wit's end, yelling at her children when they don't listen, slamming doors in frustration, striking the counter while striking fear into their hearts. And the dinner table becomes a place to avoid as opposed to a place to gather.

A fellow parent shared this about these moments:

> It took me years to recognize the pain I caused. Maybe it's better to say it took me years to come to terms with it—I always knew it was there but was too much of a coward to admit it.
>
> When I was in a room, my kids always wanted to be somewhere else. Now, I try to cover up all the pain with something different: joy, happiness—but it takes so much of that to overshadow the anxiety and fear.

While our homes are the first place we should tend to our colors, our words have far-reaching implications. They affect every relationship we have. From workplaces to coffee shops and restaurants to houses of worship, every building we set foot in and every person we meet is affected by the colors with which we choose to paint.

Jesus had this to say to the Pharisees, a group of men who often used words and religion as weapons of fear and manipulation:

> I tell you that everyone will have to give account on the day of judgment for every *empty word* they have spoken. For by your words you will be *acquitted*, and by your words you will be *condemned*.
>
> MATTHEW 12:36-37, EMPHASIS ADDED

The phrase *empty word* comes from the Greek *rhema argos*, which means careless or unprofitable words. Jesus is warning the Pharisees, all who are present, and readers for centuries to come that our words have consequences, particularly careless words that bring no good into the world.

But he doesn't stop there. Jesus drives the point home as he says, "By your words you will be *acquitted*, and by your words you will be *condemned*."

To be condemned is to be held captive, imprisoned. To be acquitted is to be set free.

Our tongues have the power to bind us or set us free. And those who receive our words experience the same captivity or freedom. We can see the evidence of this on the faces and in the hearts of those closest to us. Are we holding them captive with anger, fear, and pain? Or are we setting them free with love, joy, grace, and mercy?

What if we all chose to approach life like it was a massive book filled with tens of thousands of pages, each day a canvas with black lines delineating the events that unfold, all the things we can't foresee, the situations we can't control? And what if we lived with the understanding that our words and actions determine the colors that fill in the empty spaces of each canvas?

> **Our tongues have the power to bind us or set us free. And those that receive our words experience the same captivity or freedom.**

Our canvases are sometimes filled with bright blues and greens, oranges and yellows—colors made with soft and steady strokes, patient and deliberate, seeking to bring beauty to the world around us. These are the days when we take time to listen to those around us, seeking to understand what they are saying rather than simply waiting to respond with what we think they should do, think, feel, or believe. These are the days when the people we work with know they can trust our intentions, and our friends know we have their backs. These are the days when our children know how much we love them and are encouraged to think for themselves. And these are the days when our wives know we would do anything for them and that nothing will ever change that.

But then there are the days when our canvases are filled with angry reds, varying shades of gray, and strokes of black. Haphazard blotches of these dark colors accentuate the hard parts of the day, and jagged lines shatter the possibility for anything beautiful to be painted. These are the days when we listen to respond, when we glean just enough information to solidify an argument or perspective that we are more than ready to shove down someone's throat. These are the days when the darkness inside us rises to the surface. These are the days when the people we work with wonder if they can trust us, and our friends look for somewhere else to be. These are the days when our children avoid us, and our wives are given reason to question our motives.

> The outcome of every day's canvas is determined by the colors and brushstrokes of the words we choose. And our paintings often influence the canvases of others.

Everyone has these types of days, the good and the bad. But most days are a combination of the two—happy, joyful, sincere, loving, grace-filled, and forgiving colors mixed with angry, bitter, selfish, entitled, cruel, and arrogant ones. We're human, which means we're flawed and we're going to screw up, but it also means we have a choice.

The outcome of every day's canvas is determined by the colors and brushstrokes of the words we choose. And our paintings often influence the canvases of others. When we use dark colors, choosing hate or fear, others are more inclined to do the same; when we use bright colors, speaking words of strength and love, we give others reasons and motivation to fill their world with colors of joy.

Every day we bring beauty or pain into the lives of our children, partners, friends, neighbors, employees, and coworkers.

The words we use color the world around us.

Choose your colors wisely.

Heaven or Hell

4

Both heaven and hell are within us.

– Mahatma Gandhi

Don't search for heaven and hell in the future. Both are now present. Whenever we manage to love without expectations, calculations, negotiations, we are indeed in heaven. Whenever we fight, hate, we are in hell.

– Shams Tabrizi

You can walk by a building a thousand times and never really notice it until, one day, it jumps out at you. Our friend Seth Haines recently had this experience with a familiar building in his hometown of Fayetteville, Arkansas.

As Seth passed the Old Bank of Fayetteville Building, he finally noticed it for all its beauty and grandeur. It was as if he was seeing the Romanesque and Queen Anne–influenced building for the first time. He writes, "Good architecture sneaks up on you, I think. The building you've passed 1,000 times waits for the right moment, the right light, the right balance of elements and then, WHAMMO! she whops you upside the head and says 'Pay attention!'"

Scripture can do the same thing.

———

Since we were young boys, we have heard and recited the Lord's Prayer thousands of times. Admittedly, it often felt like it had lost its meaning, or maybe it never really meant all that much to us because we didn't appreciate it for what it is. Like so many things in life, the ones we are most familiar with are the things we value the least. Until, WHAMMO! The right situation, the right person, the right perspective wakes you up to the beauty sitting right in front of you.

> **Like so many things in life, the ones we are most familiar with are the things we value the least. Until, WHAMMO! The right situation, the right person, the right perspective wakes you up to the beauty sitting right in front of you.**

Our Lord's Prayer moment came in the middle of a sermon we heard a few years ago. We have no idea what the main topic of the sermon was, but we found the power of the message on a rabbit trail. Off on a seemingly random tangent, the pastor proceeded to dissect the Lord's Prayer, looking at each phrase individually.

Traditionally we know it as the verses found in Matthew 6:9-13:

Our Father who art in heaven, hallowed be thy name.
Thy kingdom come, thy will be done, on earth as it is in
heaven. Give us this day our daily bread; and forgive us our
debts, as we also have forgiven our debtors; and lead us
not into temptation, but deliver us from evil. (RSV)

After reading this passage, the pastor said, "So, what does each phrase mean? If we were to say this prayer today in the words we normally use, how would it sound? Turn to your neighbor and put it in your own words."

He looked around as a murmur of voices filled the room. After a few minutes, he got everyone's attention, "All right. Think about what you said to each other. What did you think of?" He let this second question hang in our minds. After a long pause, he continued, "God, you are most holy. May your love be known here on earth as it is in heaven. Be our provision in all things, and help us love others as you have loved us. Guide our paths, and be our Deliverer."

WHAMMO! It felt like a two-by-four to the forehead, but without the pain. The verses suddenly had so much to offer. As in so much of the Bible, there is a lot going on here. We could break down every aspect of these words—the fact that Jesus is teaching the disciples how to pray, what it means to be most holy, the implications of God being our provision in all things, and what it means for him to be our Deliverer. But for us, the most revolutionary parts of this ancient prayer were:

may your love be known here on earth as it is in heaven

and

help us love others as you have loved us.

For most of our lives, we have been taught that heaven is a destination, a place we go when we die—as long as we're right with God, having confessed our sins and forgiven those who have wronged us. But this piece of Scripture points to a depth Jesus is calling his followers into, an understanding that many of us fail to achieve.

We believe heaven is a place we will one day reach, but "on earth as it is in heaven" suggests there is something more. Jesus is telling us that heaven is not only a destination, but it is also an existence here and now; and we can be the very place where heaven and earth intersect. Because if we grab onto the idea that we can be vessels of God's love, and we pray for his kingdom of love to be made as real here on earth as it is in heaven, then it stands to reason that this love will be made known through us. But how?

> **Jesus is telling us that heaven is not only a destination, but it is also an existence here and now; and we can be the very place where heaven and earth intersect.**

Strip religion away and look at who Jesus was—a man who was filled with mercy, offered love and grace, and treated others with compassion regardless of religion, race, or social standing. When we approach the people in our lives the same way, striving to show them that same mercy, love, grace, and compassion, we get a glimpse of heaven, and so do they. Loving others without agenda or expectation is the only way we can participate in "on earth as it is in heaven."

But if we can experience heaven on earth, we can also bring hell into the lives of the people we encounter.

If, as many theologians agree, hell is the absence of God, and God is love, then hell must be the absence of love. When we act out of greed or anger, fuel hatred, and breed contempt, our behavior is devoid of love. And those who are on the receiving end of our actions get a glimpse of hell.

We can be the very place where heaven intersects with earth, or we can bring hell into the world of every person we meet. It all rests on our actions and motivations.

———

A friend once told us a story about a young businessman. This ambitious young man pursued new clients with fervor and rapidly built an impressive portfolio with many high-dollar accounts. His success was unparalleled. But a few years into his career, he came into work one day to find he had lost his biggest account. No reason was given, no history of the client being unhappy with the service they received; the client just canceled the account without warning.

The young man combed through all his communications with the client, reviewed meeting minutes, and replayed conversation after conversation in his head. After hours of examining his work, he came to the conclusion that he had done everything right. Frustrated, he requested a meeting with his much older and more experienced supervisor and business mentor.

As he sat across the table from the man who had taught him so much, the young man explained everything. The older gentleman sat quietly as his young protégé concluded, "I guess the adage is true; you can lead a horse to water, but you can't make it drink."

His supervisor leaned back in his chair, folded his hands behind his head, and cracked a knowing smile.

"What?" the young man asked.

"It will if it's thirsty," the supervisor replied.

"What do you mean?"

The mentor leaned forward and looked the young man in the eyes. "Your job isn't to make people drink; your job is to make them thirsty."

How often do we fall into this trap, convincing ourselves it's our job to make people drink? It's the fatal flaw of many churches and the Achilles' heel of anyone who chooses religion over relationship. When we focus on making people drink our beliefs, our point of view, or a set of rules, as opposed to making them thirsty for more love, grace, and mercy, we have lost sight of the truth of Jesus' words—"on earth as it is in heaven." Heaven is distant, and hell is lurking in the shadows of our misguided intentions.

Different versions of hell on earth play out every day, from the playgrounds in our neighborhoods to countries in the developing world.

We see it when parents, absorbed in their phones, dismiss their children. As the little people they have brought into the world propel themselves on swings or climb rope ladders on the playground and shout, "Come play with me," Mom and Dad ignore the pleas for attention and time—and those young minds begin to question their value.

We hear it when a driver stops at a busy intersection and notices the unwashed clothes and duct-taped shoes of a man panhandling on the corner. As the driver waits for the light to turn green, he leans out the window to let the homeless man know what he thinks of him: "Why don't you get a job? Have some self-respect."

We know it when social media explodes over politics or religion, and so many are quick to spew words of anger, hate, and destruction, turning Scripture into a weapon of division instead of a vehicle of love.

We feel it when we learn of atrocities happening far and wide. When men and women are ostracized and beaten because their faith or ideals differ from the majority. When people celebrate the murder of forty-nine people at a gay bar, claiming God's judgment. When families starve and children die because governments withhold food and aid.

While a child ignored on the playground is a far cry from one dying of starvation, both feel pain, and both long to be loved. Hell on earth is everywhere, but we can fight back, we can press against the shadows. Darkness always gives way to light.

Heaven on earth is everywhere.

We see it when parents set aside their phones and meetings, making time to push their children on the swings or chase them through the playground. Children know their value when a mother closes her eyes, counts to ten, and yells with laughter, "Ready or not, here I come."

We hear it when someone sits down next to the homeless man

panhandling on the corner and asks, "Are you hungry?" and together they break bread; someone who is so lonely suddenly isn't alone.

We know it when social media campaigns and posts elevate those that many in our society see as lesser, and when men and women take a stand against misogyny, homophobia, and racism.

We feel it when we learn of organizations putting fresh water wells in Africa; nonprofits providing food, clothing, and education to young kids who would otherwise never have them; and volunteers offering love and support in the face of natural disasters regardless of a person's race, religion, or sexual orientation.

> We must recognize *on earth as it is in heaven* can only happen when we love others the same way God loves us— completely, without agenda or expectation, just as we are; it's the only way darkness will yield.

When we love others without agenda or expectation, setting our differing beliefs and understandings aside, valuing them merely because they are human, because they are God's creations, we bring heaven to earth.

The two of us will never look at Matthew 6:9-13 the same. While it will always be known as the Lord's Prayer, to us it is now so much more than a prayer. It is a calling, a challenge, a mantra by which we try to live.

How do we embrace the existence God has called us to? We must recognize *on earth as it is in heaven* can only happen when we love others the same way God loves us—completely, without agenda or expectation, just as we are; it's the only way darkness will yield. When we bring heaven into the lives of those we meet, they will follow suit, joining us on the journey.

Together, we can fight the darkness—but only if we choose the light.

Contagious

5

A healthy attitude is contagious, but don't wait to catch it from others. Be a carrier.

– Tom Stoppard

OUR LIVES ARE FILLED WITH PEOPLE who have shaped who we have become. Our parents showed us how to love, taught us to tell right from wrong, and introduced us to our faith. Friends and mentors have helped grow and shape that faith. And our wives have loved us because of and in spite of who we are. Every person who is or ever has been a part of our lives possesses strength, wisdom, and resiliency that we look to as a guide for living life.

Sometimes it's easy to think that our influence is limited to our families and our circle of friends. But we don't affect just those we hold close. Who we are has cascading effects on everyone we meet. Like stones thrown into a pond, our words and behaviors leave ripples in every moment of life.

Every day, we make decisions that impact those we encounter. Often, the effects of the choices we make go unnoticed by us, but someone is always watching. The way we deal with difficult phone calls affects the children who overhear our raised voices. Our demeanor can change a happy moment into an experience filled with stress. A dismissive attitude toward the barista at a coffee shop can ruin their day. Not only do we have the ability to negatively impact our environment and the lives of those we encounter, our decisions can also influence the choices of others. Whether we like it or not, our behaviors are contagious. Others often mimic or respond to who we choose to be—hate begets hate, fear begets fear, pain begets pain.

> **Like stones thrown into a pond, our words and behaviors leave ripples in every moment of life.**

We see this every day in social media posts about politics or religion. One person spews words of hate, minimizing the existence of another human being or an entire group of people, and others join in. The lemming mentality humanity is prone to runs rampant when we get caught up in negativity and hate.

But the opposite is also true—when we approach stressful situations with grace and dignity, others are more inclined to do the same. We can choose to be light and love even in the face of hard situations. And when we approach life and the people we encounter with compassion, that same love will flourish in the lives of others.

———

Jerry McConnell is a part-time pastor for the senior adults at our local church. Before retirement, he spent forty years in full-time ministry, filling every capacity a pastor could. A lifetime of working in the church setting brought Jerry face-to-face with every situation imaginable—love and heartache, the beauty of life, the hardships of death. He officiated weddings, conducted funerals, and counseled marriages—some made it, others didn't. He held the hands of men and women as they died, and he welcomed newborn babies into the world.

A career filled with baptisms, dedications, and eulogies exposed Jerry to a host of joys and pains—and he learned a lot of lessons along the way. But perhaps the most significant lesson occurred after his retirement and in a capacity much different than working within the walls of a church.

Shortly after Jerry left full-time ministry, he fell into a unique second career. In 2008, the Center for Personal Protection and Safety (CPPS) approached him regarding a job opportunity.

CPPS is an organization that specializes in keeping employees of organizations safe in the workplace and while traveling abroad, and they were branching out in their client base. Seeing a potential need in the faith-based sector, CPPS hired Jerry to interface with churches and to service these types of accounts as the senior adviser of their ministry outreach and non-profit division.

Jerry was soon conducting safety discussions and trainings for church employees from across the country. Representatives of denominations and faith communities far and wide came to CPPS's home city of Spokane, Washington, to participate and learn from one another. It was at one of these trainings that he met Bob Johnson.

Bob spent twenty years in the Arizona Army National Guard, retired from the Phoenix Police Department after twenty-three years of service, and spent ten years working as a detective for the Organized Crime Bureau. On paper, Bob sounds like the ultimate tough guy, and he may be, but he also has a heart for people.

As director of safety and security at Christ's Church of the Valley in Peoria, Arizona, Bob was an obvious choice to attend the discussions at CPPS. From the moment they met, Jerry and Bob hit it off, and a friendship began to develop.

From 2008 to 2011, Bob and other clientele continued to fly to

Spokane to get their necessary training, but as CPPS grew and their client base expanded, Jerry's role evolved to meet the demand. Churches across the country began requesting onsite training and advisement, and Jerry realized that he needed help if he was going to be successful. He needed an additional trainer, and Bob Johnson was the perfect fit.

On their first business trip together, the duo found themselves on a flight to Garland, Texas, to work with an area church. Jerry thought he had gotten to know Bob reasonably well over the three years since they'd met, but there was a depth to Bob's character he had yet to see.

When they landed at the airport, Jerry and Bob headed to the rental car counter, where Bob handled the pickup. Jerry watched as his friend engaged with the clerk—a young man in his twenties who avoided eye contact and spoke softly, and whose disheveled appearance gave the impression that life wasn't what he had hoped it would be. Bob smiled at the clerk and said, "How are you doing today?"

Without looking up, the young man said in a soft yet irritated tone, "How can I help you?"

Bob looked at the man's name tag, called him by name, and began a conversation that disarmed the quiet, cold presentation.

The conversation lasted for only a few minutes, but during those few moments it was like that young man was the only person in the world that mattered.

Jerry watched as his colleague talked with the clerk at the rental car counter like they were long-lost friends. The conversation lasted for only a few minutes, but during those few moments it was like that young man was the only person in the world that mattered to Bob. When they left, the clerk smiled and thanked both Jerry and Bob for being customers.

As they walked to their car, Jerry briefly thought, "That was nice of Bob." He appreciated how Bob had approached the young man with love and compassion, but he didn't think much more of it.

When they arrived at their hotel, Jerry and Bob parked their rental car in the hotel lot, gathered their bags, and headed inside to get keys to their rooms. At the reception desk, what Jerry had witnessed earlier happened all over again, but this time to a much greater degree.

Bob noticed the check-in clerk's name badge and wedding ring, and said, "Chris, how long have you been married?"

"A couple of years," Chris replied, a smile spreading across his face.

Bob smiled back. "Any kids?"

"Not yet, but we're planning on it."

The conversation continued, and Jerry watched Bob make Chris light up as they talked about the joys of marriage, the prospect of kids, and what Chris enjoyed about his job.

As Bob handed Chris his company card, Chris said, "I get to meet a lot of great people."

"I bet you do," Bob replied.

"What brings you to Garland?" Chris asked as he programmed the room key cards.

"We're in town for work, but we need a favor. This is our first time in Garland, and we have a rule that when we travel, we can't eat at a restaurant that we can find at home. What's your favorite place to grab a bite?"

Looking up, Chris said, "There are several my wife and I enjoy."

Bob nodded. "Okay, imagine it's your anniversary—where would you take your wife?"

A smile spread across Chris's face. "That's easy. There is a great local steak house we love, a little pricey but amazing food."

"Perfect! Is there one dish we have to get?"

Handing Bob his credit card and the room keys, Chris said, "You can't go wrong with the fillet."

Bob wrote down the name of the restaurant, got directions, and finished the conversation with, "How late are you working tonight?"

"Eleven."

"Great, maybe we will see you after dinner."

After dropping off their bags in their rooms, Jerry and Bob headed to the steak house. Within minutes of their arrival, Bob knew both the greeter at the door and the hostess by name. So when they were seated and began to peruse the menu, Jerry wasn't surprised when Bob began talking with the young woman who approached the table like they were long-lost friends.

Jerry ordered his meal, and the server turned to Bob. "And for you, sir?"

After Bob ordered a steak, he said, "If it's okay, we're going to need two tabs. The company will pay for our two meals, but I would like a beer with my steak, and I need to place an order to go."

"No problem," the young woman said with a smile.

"Great! Could I get the fillet as well, but please don't have it ready until we are wrapping up? Just put it in a to-go box if you would."

The server headed toward the kitchen to put in the order. Jerry stared at Bob, wondering what in the world he was up to.

On the drive back to the hotel, Jerry indicated the meal in Bob's lap and asked, "What are you planning on doing with that?" Bob just smiled.

As they walked into the lobby of the hotel, Jerry watched as Bob approached the reception desk, where Chris was still working.

Chris smiled. "How was it?" Looking down at the large box in Bob's hands, he commented, "That's a lot of leftovers."

"These aren't leftovers." Bob handed Chris the container.

With a confused look on his face, Chris said, "What's this?"

"It's the fillet. I figured you could use a good meal on a night like tonight. Have a good evening." And with a smile and a wave, Bob walked toward the elevators.

That was in 2011. Jerry and Bob have been working together ever since, and Jerry has seen his friend treat people like this hundreds of times over the years. Sometimes the interactions last thirty seconds, others four or five minutes, but Bob always leaves an impression. And not just on the people behind rental car counters, at hotel reception desks, or restaurants; Bob has left an impression on Jerry.

When asked about Bob's influence on him, Jerry replied,

You've probably heard the quote, "I'd rather see a sermon than hear one any day." That's what Bob has done for me; he has literally changed the way I interact with total strangers on a daily basis because I witnessed it—I saw somebody do it so effortlessly and give so much joy to others. I thought, "I'm going to try that. I want to do that."

This is how much he has impacted my life—one day I got up in the morning knowing I had to be out and about most of the day, and I asked myself, "How many times can I be Bob Johnson today?"

Thirteen.

Thirteen times that day I had those kinds of moments—with grocery store clerks, people at the coffee shop, the library, you name it. I lay in bed that night and replayed every one of them, every single scenario. And I had this stupid grin on my face as I just thought about how it changed people's eyes, their faces, their countenances.

I asked Bob after I had witnessed him in action a few times, "I love what you do, but why? Where does this come from?"

He said, "I heard a sermon one time where the pastor quoted Ephesians, saying Jesus went about doing good. You know, I've never been to Bible college, I've never been to seminary, but I can do that. I can encourage, love, and meet people's needs. I can speak joy, and hope, and life into a person and watch them come alive."

Bob's goal is to be like Jesus everywhere he goes. And now, so is mine.

But it doesn't stop there. Bob's way of living has spread from me to others, including my wife. Now she does the same things, seeing people as a destination for the love, time, and resources she has, looking for opportunities to show love in every interaction.

———

What would the world look like if we approached each person we encounter by looking them in the eye and treating them with kindness and respect?

In the Bible, a man known as Joseph was renamed by the apostles because he went about doing good. Barnabas was the name they gave him. In Hebrew, Barnabas means Son of Encouragement.

Like Barnabas, Bob Johnson has chosen to be a son of encouragement. He and so many others we know make the conscious decision to be light and love to everyone they encounter. And like a disease spreading through contact, this kind of behavior is infectious, but everyone who witnesses it *wants* to catch it.

An army of hate-filled people can cause so much damage and perpetuate so much fear. But what would an army of Bob Johnsons accomplish? What would the world look like if we approached each person we encounter by looking them in the eye and treating them with kindness and respect? How much joy could we spread, how much light could we give, and how many others would follow?

Bob Johnson is one man in a sea of many, and yet he has touched more lives than he will ever know through a simple decision and the understanding that what he does and who he is each day is contagious. He paints the world with beauty and chooses heaven every day.

We all can profoundly affect each relationship we are a part of and each person we meet, for better or worse.

Who you are is contagious—make sure you're worth catching!

Flowers

6

The world is awaiting your gift—all you have to do is show up with the right intention!

– Lewis Howes

GIFT GIVING IS A PART OF LIFE. Birthdays, weddings, anniversaries, Christmas, Mother's Day, Father's Day, Valentine's Day—there are many reasons to give something special to the people we love. Sometimes we put a lot of thought into choosing a specific gift. But other times, we go with the safe bet—flowers.

Appropriate for so many occasions, flowers are the most common gift given to people when they're ill. The simple beauty of their petals, the variety of colors they bring to a room, and their subtle fragrances have brightened many a dark day.

No matter the gifts we receive, there is always intention behind them—love, affection, thanks, the notion that someone is thinking about us. But sometimes, a simple gift winds up being much more than a bouquet of flowers.

———

Hospitals are busy places. The halls are filled with people headed to and fro—to X-ray, from the lab, to chemotherapy, from surgery, to outpatient appointments, from the delivery room—so many destinations, for patients dealing with a host of different challenges. In a hospital you're guaranteed to meet people from all walks of life and encounter stories of all kinds: happy ones, sad ones, planned ones, unexpected ones.

A vital part of every hospital is its staff—people who've chosen careers grounded in caring for others. Physicians use their knowledge and training to treat diseases of all types; nurses and aides work hour after hour at bedsides, distributing medications, monitoring and assessing patients, and providing hands-on care. Teams of people transport patients to a variety of locations for things like CAT scans and MRIs; administrators manage the staff and oversee the placement of patients. Emergency room staff triage the unexpected admissions, and other employees work behind the scenes, managing medical records, maintaining the building and grounds, and making sure everyone in a hospital bed is fed.

Some of the most incredible people you will find in hospitals aren't the paid staff—they're the volunteers, men and women who choose to spend time with patients, delivering flowers and balloons, dropping off letters, and carrying out tasks of all types just to make sure things run smoothly.

But some of the most incredible people you will find in hospitals aren't the paid staff—they're the volunteers, men and women who choose to spend time with patients, delivering flowers and balloons, dropping off letters, and carrying out tasks of all types just to make sure things run smoothly.

As a lifelong patient and a former healthcare administrator, we have both met many volunteers. Most of them are retired—men and women who have spent years in a variety of careers but now devote part of their well-deserved permanent break from full-time work to helping others when things aren't turning out as planned. One of these volunteers was named Betty.

Having spent years as a grade-school teacher, Betty was no stranger to helping others. For thirty-plus years she poured into the lives of children, teaching them how to read and write, and the importance of math. Each week she offered young boys and girls a safe place to learn, a place where they knew they were loved and valued.

When she wasn't tending to the growth of young children, Betty offered nurture of a different kind. Betty had a passion for gardening. She would tend to a variety of fruits and vegetables each spring and summer, but her real knack was with flowers. Snapdragons, roses, tulips, daffodils, and many others grew in her beds and pots, but her favorites were lilies. She loved their pure beauty and delicate appearance.

As she grew older, Betty's knees and back began to feel her age as she struggled to manage the sizable plants in her yard. So she turned to the variety of pots and beds that populated the small greenhouse her husband had built for her before he passed. One of his last gifts to her before he died was the ability to enjoy the colors and fragrances of her beloved flowers long after she left the classroom.

After she retired, Betty began spending more time in her greenhouse, but her plants only needed so many hours of care. She felt idle and needed something to fill her time, but she didn't want another hobby; she missed working with people. At the recommendation of a friend, Betty applied to volunteer at a local hospital.

Within days, she fell in love with the work. Sometimes she would sort papers or build patient education folders; other days she found herself escorting the families of patients through the confusing halls of the hospital. But Betty's favorite task was delivering the variety of gifts that arrived for patients. Balloons, cookie bouquets, potted plants, and flowers came in every day, and Betty jumped at the chance to be the one to take them to patient rooms.

But one thing she couldn't stand was the thought of someone spending time in the hospital with no get-well gift. Betty soon began to put together bouquets of flowers from her greenhouse for the patients she met who seemed to have few visitors or no gifts to speak of.

Each week, Betty would note which patients could use a bit of cheering up and made a point to bring flowers to brighten their day. Her creations found their way to the pediatric unit, labor and delivery, and each of the variety of medical and surgical floors.

Betty always arrived on time and ready to work her shift because she loved working with and meeting so many beautiful people. Some were broken from loss, others excited for a new future. But all seemed to find a little bit of joy when Betty came to their room. Every person she met had a place in her heart, but several years into her second career of volunteering, Betty encountered a very special patient.

On her way to deliver some flowers to an elderly patient on the orthopedic floor, Betty walked to the front desk to double-check the room number. She overheard some nurses discussing a patient who was particularly down, and no one knew why. Betty took a mental note, delivered the flowers, and continued about her day.

The next morning, she put together a small bouquet of lilies and drove to the hospital early to make her special delivery to the orthopedic floor. She checked with the patient's nurse to make sure flowers were okay and headed down the hall.

Knocking on the door to the room, Betty said, "Good morning. May I come in? I have a delivery for you."

"Come in," came the reply.

Betty stepped into the room and found herself staring into the eyes of a young woman who appeared to be in her early thirties. Her long, black hair was pulled back in a ponytail, and her blue eyes starkly contrasted with the pale hospital gown she wore.

The young woman's stare shifted from Betty's face to the flowers she held in her hands. Betty introduced herself and explained, "I'm a volunteer here, and I wanted to bring you some flowers."

The woman continued to stare at the flowers. "How did you know?"

"How did I know what?" Betty replied.

"That lilies are my favorite," the patient said, a quiver in her voice.

"I didn't, but they're my favorite too."

When she finally broke her gaze from the flowers, the woman asked, "What did you say your name was?"

"Betty. And yours?"

"Karen," she said softly.

"Karen, it is a pleasure to meet you. Is there somewhere you would prefer I put your flowers?"

Karen reached for her bedside table, adjusted it so it sat over her lap, and said, "Here. I want them right here so I can see them up close." She paused for a few moments and then said, "I can't believe you brought me lilies. You're sure no one told you?"

"I'm sure; I just overheard that you could use some cheering up, and I have a greenhouse full of flowers that I love to share with patients."

"You have no idea what this means to me. Do you have a moment to talk? I want to tell you a story."

Betty sat next to the bed and listened as Karen told her the story of her youngest daughter.

"When she was six years old, she developed leukemia. We

tried every treatment we could—chemo, radiation, experimental medications—nothing worked. The cancer slowly worked its way through her body—she died a year after her diagnosis. My husband and I have two other kids, an older son and daughter. We're a happy family, most of the time, but my kids miss their sister." Karen paused to compose herself and grabbed a tissue to dab her eyes. "My husband and I, we miss our daughter. It's been four years, and I can still see her face as clear as day." Karen laughed to herself. "Her name was Lily. My husband and I, we often take lilies to her."

> **When our motivations are pure and we act accordingly, someone's life will undoubtedly be made better.**

Karen reached over to Betty, grabbed her hand, and squeezed it gently. "Thank you so much for this. This is one of the greatest gifts I've ever received. They're exactly what I needed right now."

Betty smiled with tears in her eyes. "You're so very welcome. Thank you for telling me about Lily."

The two women sat together as Karen shared more about her family. They laughed and cried, and when the conversation came to a close, Betty stood up, hugged Karen, and said, "It was wonderful to meet you."

"You too, Betty. You have made this a wonderful day."

———

Sometimes a small thing, given with the simplest of intentions, ends up being so much more. Betty was blessed to be able to see this firsthand, but most of us will never know the weight of our actions. However, that doesn't make them any less important. When our motivations are pure and we act accordingly, someone's life will undoubtedly be made better.

Karen's world was made better because of a small thing given with pure intentions. Betty brought joy into her world with a simple gift, motivated by the desire to show love and compassion to another human being.

We all have a gift to share. What are your flowers?

Bending Time

7

Time and memory are true artists; they remould reality nearer to the heart's desire.

– John Dewey

ALBERT EINSTEIN WAS BORN on March 14, 1879, in the city of Ulm, in what was then the German Empire. From an early age, he demonstrated an aptitude for mathematics and physics, soon reaching an understanding far beyond that of his peers. At twelve, Einstein developed a passion for geometry and algebra and started teaching himself advanced mathematics, and by age fourteen, he had mastered integral and differential calculus.

Understanding and applying existing branches of science and math weren't enough for Einstein; he needed to create new ones to explain the unexplainable. As a result, he developed a host of theories throughout his scientific career that would eventually revolutionize our understanding of mathematics and physics. Perhaps his most famous ones are his theories of relativity.

One of those is the theory of general relativity. His widely accepted idea is essentially a geometric theory of gravity and is the foundation for the current description and understanding of gravity in physics. The details can be explained by complex mathematics, but suffice it to say that general relativity defines gravity as a geometric property of space and time.

It's because of Einstein's ideas that scientists suspected the existence of black holes, areas in space where a powerful gravitational force so heavily distorts space and time that nothing can escape, not even light. When this happens, different points of space and time can be brought together, or so the theory goes. If you're like us, this is a bit difficult to conceptualize, but you're wondering what it might look like.

Picture a blanket, drawn tight at the corners. When you drop a marble on the fabric, there's little effect. The marble bounces while the blanket doesn't seem to move at all. But drop a bowling ball on the blanket, and the force draws areas of fabric toward the point of impact, bringing otherwise distant sections of the fabric very close together—so close they might even touch.

Life is not so different. But swap out the bowling ball for everyday encounters and occurrences, and trade the blanket for the fabric of our lives—a tapestry made up of all our memories and histories, the events that have made us who we are.

———

The two of us have traveled all over the world together, and it never ceases to amaze us how our senses can take us back to specific places or replay distant experiences in our minds. Each time we walk by a bakery with baguettes, the aroma of the fresh warm bread sparks memories of strolling down a side street in Paris with our wives. The cafés con leche at Azúcar in San Diego transport us to any of the cafés along the Camino de Santiago in Spain. And any song from Muse's album *Origin of Symmetry* has us reminiscing about our trip to Europe in 2001 where we first discovered the band in a small record store in Munich.

The human mind is an incredible creation; it can learn things as complicated as physics or calculus, catalog scientific facts, comprehend complex analogies, and create beautiful works of fiction or stunning pieces of art. And yet, in the blink of an eye, the notes of a song, the flavor of a cup of coffee, or the aroma of fresh-baked bread can hijack whatever is going on inside our heads and take us to a place we haven't thought about in weeks, months, or even years.

> In the blink of an eye, the notes of a song, the flavor of a cup of coffee, or the aroma of fresh-baked bread can hijack whatever is going on inside our heads and take us to a place we haven't thought about in weeks, months, or even years.

Childhood was a wonderful time for the two of us—years filled with having friends over for dinner, sleepovers on weekends or holiday breaks, birthday parties, and adventures in the fields beyond our homes. We went camping and hiking, rode our bikes across town, and swam at the community pool on hot summer days. And now that we are both parents, the joy continues when one of our children has a friend over after school, builds a fort in the garage with a neighbor, climbs a tree with their siblings, or experiences something new on vacation. Every day they are creating memories, much like we did as kids.

If you listen to the young ones in your life, rarely does a day go by where the words, "do you remember . . .", "that reminds me of . . .", or "last time we . . ." aren't a part of their conversations. They're excited to recall the fun games they create and the adventures they find themselves on.

But kids aren't just keeping track of the good times. Fights with brothers and sisters, altercations on the playground with a bully, and moments where they feel unjustly disciplined are tracked inside their minds—sometimes subconsciously, but rest assured, those memories are there.

Children process their life experiences every second of every day. Each moment finds its way into a mental catalogue of situations stored somewhere inside the brain, and each of those memories can be recalled at a moment's notice and sometimes without warning.

———

Maggie grew up in a typical neighborhood filled with boys and girls her age running down the streets, riding bikes in the culs-de-sac, and playing hide-and-seek late into summer evenings. Every night she rested her head on a pillow in her own room, where she had a bed that kept her warm on cold winter nights. There was always food on the table and clothes on her back.

Maggie's mother cared for her and her brother and sister with love and compassion, making sure their needs were met, teaching them right from wrong, and nurturing them through each stage of life. Maggie's relationships with her mom, brother, and sister brought desperately needed stability to her world—because Maggie's father was far from stable. He drank—a lot. He was depressed most of the time. And he saw little good in the life he lived or the family he was supposed to love.

Though Maggie's dad never laid a hand on her, her eighteen years at home were filled with verbal and emotional abuse, words of the worst kind about her worth or lack thereof. She and her siblings suffered all types of fear and insecurity even as their mother tried to protect them. Family vacations were things to try to forget rather than cherished memories. Driving lessons turned into lessons about how stupid the children were. Neither Maggie nor her siblings could do anything right in the eyes of their hatred-filled father. And the wounds created by years of hostility and rage were deep.

In college, Maggie fell in love with a young man whom she eventually married. Steven was nothing like Maggie's father, but he knew more than he cared to about the man.

Like any couple, Steven and Maggie had disagreements where angry words were exchanged and apologies were needed. In the heat of one argument, Steven lost his temper, raised his voice far more than necessary, and yelled at Maggie in frustration and anger. Her face, filled with indignation just a moment before, was suddenly overcome with fear. Convulsing sobs overtook her as Steven looked on, confused by the drastic change in his wife.

Things calmed down, apologies were accepted, and the couple began to unpack what had just happened. They decided to go to counseling, and Steven soon learned that though he hadn't uttered a single word about Maggie's worth, his anger-filled voice and seemingly uncontrolled temper had taken her back in time to a moment when her father stood over her and unleashed his rage. Steven's behavior had caused Maggie's worst memories to surface.

> **Events of magnitude often come with a rush of emotion. Whether good or bad, they have the power to take us back to situations or experiences from years before as the past and present collide.**

————

Events of magnitude often come with a rush of emotion. Whether good or bad, they have the power to take us back to situations or experiences from years before as the past and present collide.

Some people have been lucky enough to be raised in a healthy home, escaping the one-in-four chance of abuse, the trauma of neglect, and having to wonder where their next meal would come from. Most of the memories these people can recall are good ones. But there are a lot of children out there who haven't been so fortunate—life lived on the streets; physical, emotional, or sexual abuse; the tragic loss of siblings or parents. Their memories are filled with pain, fear, and insecurity.

And those children become adults, the men and women you meet on a daily basis. Men and women whose lives are made up of more sadness than joy. The question we have to ask ourselves is, will we be the ones who remind them of the pain in their lives, or will we be the ones to bring the few bright spots of their years on earth to the surface while making new ones they can return to in the future?

While time machines haven't been invented yet, we do have the ability to "travel through time." A moment right here, right now, can come face-to-face with the beauty or pain of something that happened years ago. Just as the right flavor, aroma, or sound can take us back to places in our distant past, our actions, when filled with compassion and love, can take others "back in time" to cherished moments and favored memories.

And when we behave out of anger and frustration, we can transport someone back in time to their episodes of trauma, abuse, and pain.

This is a challenging notion, because it means our responsibility for our behavior extends far beyond how it affects us. Our words and actions have incredible power and, whether we admit it or not, each one of us has taken others back to places they didn't want to be. Our words, actions, and intentions have been vehicles through which things better left in the past came rushing into the present.

Each of us is a time machine, possessing the power to transport others to specific moments, based on how we choose to collide with the fabric of their lives. Like a wrecking ball, our darkness can crash into their world, bringing a host of painful moments into the here and now—or our light can press into their hearts, reminding them of the good things in their lives. This is why we need to choose compassion, why we should act in love, why we must be kind, and why we need to embrace mercy.

> **Each of us is a time machine, possessing the power to transport others to specific moments, based on how we choose to collide with the fabric of their lives.**

And even more than reminding someone of the good in their lives, we can be a point in space and time where someone will one day return, a moment when they knew they were loved and compassion was real, all because we gave it freely.

When the Ink Runs Out

8

Carve your name on hearts, not tombstones. A legacy is etched into the minds of others and the stories they share about you.

– Shannon L. Alder

EVERY LIFE IS FILLED WITH STORIES—tales of how we mature and grow, the lessons we learn, the mistakes we make, how we respond to joy and pain. Some of these stories take years to unfold, while others last only minutes. Pieced together, like the chapters of a book, they tell our histories.

And like the lives we choose to live, some books are better than others. Sometimes this is because the author decided to write characters in a certain way or let certain events happen, situations that draw us deeper into the pages. But the books we enjoy the most have one thing in common. As the last chapter comes to a close and the story comes to its conclusion, the best ones don't truly end. When the last bit of ink is used and the

> When the last bit of ink is used and the final word is written, the greatest stories live on with new possibilities inside the hearts and minds of their readers.

final word is written, the greatest stories live on with new possibilities inside the hearts and minds of their readers.

When life is lived like a good book and a man or woman leaves the world in a way that those left behind are better because of them—those are the greatest stories. Their legacies aren't defined by the estates or financial resources passed on to their next of kin, but rather by the beauty of the relationships they built. They live on in the lives of others because of the memories they made and the love they shared.

———

We have been blessed with many friends over the years, and we've often been lucky enough to get to know their parents as well. Rick Daniels, the father of our friend Luke, has lived a life full of good stories. Some are his; some are the stories of others. Most are a mixture of both, the result of lives colliding in beautiful ways.

Over the past few years, as we have gotten to know Rick, it has become apparent that the man is filled with wisdom. A retired army veteran and nurse practitioner, Rick has a lot of experience to share.

During his twenty-eight years in the military, Rick served in various roles and divisions, including four deployments, eventually retiring as a full-bird colonel. Amid pursuing a successful army career, Rick married and started a family.

In his late forties, Rick was working as a professor at Oregon Health and Science University in Portland, Oregon. While working in higher education was rewarding, Rick missed spending time with patients. He began to work with men and women who were on hospice, individuals facing a variety of end-of-life scenarios who needed help with their care or someone to take them to clinic appointments and treatments. It was during this time that Rick found himself connected to one particular patient through his son Luke.

The father of one of Luke's good friends had contracted non-Hodgkin's lymphoma, and though he didn't know him well, Rick chose to care for David as his disease progressed. Rick soon learned that David had served in Vietnam as a Green Beret and during his tours of duty was exposed to large amounts of Agent Orange.

Agent Orange is a defoliant and herbicide widely used during the Vietnam War for crop destruction and jungle defoliation. Agent Orange is now presumed to be a causative agent for non-Hodgkin's lymphoma.

Non-Hodgkin's lymphoma is a form of cancer that affects the body's immune system. Tumors develop in the lymph nodes and lymphatic tissues, and patients often experience abdominal pain and swelling, chest pain, persistent fatigue, fevers, and night sweats. In advanced cases, tumors metastasize or spread to other areas of the body such as the liver, lungs, or bones.

Treatments vary, but in advanced cases, radiation and chemotherapy are necessary evils. When Rick began caring for David, these aggressive treatments had become a part of David's medical regimen.

When he met him, Rick's new patient was still strong despite the disease. David stood at six foot one and weighed in at a little over two hundred pounds. With black hair and dark brown eyes that sat behind glasses, David was a quiet man who possessed a peaceful yet strong presence. After two tours in Vietnam, David served for a number of years as a police officer, and when Rick first met him, David was still hard at work. He managed the trucking division of Croman, a logging company in the area.

From the onset of their relationship, Rick wanted to help David; he had an earnest desire to serve others. But he was also fascinated by David's background in the military and his years in the Special

Forces. He figured David had some fascinating stories to tell. But what Rick learned from David ended up being very different from what he expected.

At the beginning, sick as he was, David didn't need much help. But he still welcomed the assistance Rick offered in getting him to and from his appointments and scheduled treatments. Sometimes Kathy, David's wife, would join them, but usually Rick and David would go alone. Several times a week, Rick would pick up David. They would make a quick stop for coffee and then drive to David's various chemotherapy appointments, radiation treatments, and visits with internists or oncologists, usually about twenty-five minutes each way. These car rides were the opportunity Rick had been looking for, time to get to know David's story and to hear about Vietnam.

Every drive would start the same way. Rick would ask "nurse questions," inquiring how David was feeling, looking for any new symptoms, or exploring potential side effects from chemotherapy or radiation. Once Rick was done with his check-in, David would change the subject, turning the conversation around to focus on Rick. David would ask about Rick's family, wanting to know how the kids were doing, what was new in Rick's world, making sure he was taking time for himself and spending time with his wife and kids. And with every response Rick gave, David would drill in a little bit more, looking for ways to get to know his new friend.

As the weeks passed, the two men learned more and more about each other, and their friendship grew stronger. For months they danced the same dance with every car ride and every conversation. As Rick cared for David, David looked for ways to return the favor.

Over the course of more than a year and a half, the two men grew closer, and so did their families. Kathy became good friends with Rick and his wife, Nancy; their grown kids spent time together when home from school or in town for holidays. The families often shared dinners and spent special occasions together, and their bond grew so strong that Rick and Kathy began to think of each other as brother and sister. Meanwhile, the disease worsened, cancer spread, and David faced the inevitable.

As he continued to deteriorate physically, David developed severe joint pain and struggled to walk, and parts of his body began to fail. But Rick continued to take him anywhere he needed to go. And while Rick's medical questions dealt with more severe symptoms and heavier topics, the two friends also swapped stories from the field, reflected on fatherhood, and discussed what it meant to be a husband. Rick also learned more about David's life and his time as a Green Beret.

The Army Special Forces, commonly known as the Green Berets, are formed from the best of the best. Groups of hundreds of men attempt to qualify for testing to become a Green Beret, only one hundred make it through to Green Beret training, and only three of those graduate.

Those dedicated enough to make the cut are divided into teams of twelve, and those teams are further separated into smaller groups of six. David trained as a combat medic, but a part of the Green Berets' success was that each member of the groups of six was cross-trained so they could do everyone else's job effectively. If one man fell, there was someone available to step in and do what needed to be done.

In the summer of 2003 Rick and his family had a vacation planned for July, but as June approached, David's health declined rapidly, and Rick knew his friend's time was near. Not wanting to be away when David passed, Rick and his family canceled their vacation.

When Rick told him this, David asked, "Now, why are you not going on your vacation? You need to spend time with your family."

Rick replied, "Because I want to be here."

Nothing else needed to be said. David knew why Rick was staying, and Rick knew he didn't need to spell it out.

Throughout their friendship, Rick saw David cry two times—this was one of them; the other was two weeks later when David made a special request of Rick. Ten days before he passed, with tears in his eyes, David asked Rick, "Will you do my memorial service?"

"I would be honored," Rick replied.

David smiled. "Okay, now I don't want you blubbering your way through it."

David then listed his requests for the service: Rick would be in uniform, as is the tradition at funerals for veterans; he would give the American flag to Kathy and the kids; "The Ballad of the Green Berets" would play; and Rick would speak of David's priorities in life.

Then David made another special request. David's love for his wife had been evident throughout the time Rick had known him. He'd seen the two banter back and forth, teasing each other and flirting until the end. A month before he died, David told his wife, "I want you to date when I'm gone." And he meant it. He wanted to know Kathy would be taken care of, that she wouldn't be alone. So he asked Rick if he and Nancy would give Kathy gifts on her birthday, her and David's anniversary, and Christmas. Honored to be trusted with such a responsibility, Rick said, "Of course we will."

> "What I saw as my caring for David wound up being an avenue for him to care for his wife. David made sure that as he faced death, she would have a family in us."

David passed the day after he retired, the memorial service was held, and Rick did his best to honor his friend's request and not blubber his way through it. But the weight and beauty of David's special request didn't hit Rick until several months after the funeral.

What began as a nurse caring for a patient led to a friendship where two men grew close through their shared experiences, the beauty and pain of life, and the inevitable final chapter of death. But there was something else going on over those twenty months.

With each conversation and every car ride, David was getting to know the family he would one day entrust his wife to. Reflecting on David's request, Rick said,

What I didn't know was that there was compassion at work in this relationship in three different ways. One was from me to David as I cared for him. Another was from David to me as he pursued me; he truly wanted to know me and saw me as a friend. But the third and most significant was through my family to Kathy.

I never thought of this until after he had passed, but the relationship we now have with Kathy was made possible because of David. We would never have gotten to know her the way we do or become a part of her family if it hadn't been for David's pursuing us throughout his disease process.

What I saw as my caring for David wound up being an avenue for him to care for his wife. David made sure that as he faced death, she would have a family in us.

After the funeral, we got together with Kathy, or "sis" as we call her, more and more. And in the months and years since David's passing, we've spent holidays together, celebrated birthdays, had good cries and hard conversations. We still give Kathy gifts on her birthday, her and David's anniversary, and Christmas. But really, those gifts are from David.

God orchestrated an amazing thing through David's love for his wife.

———

We do so much for those we love, but perhaps the most significant thing we can do is leave them with the best part of us when we go.

Just like the Green Berets are trained to do every man's job, David needed to know there would be someone to do his when he no longer could. During all those car ride conversations, David was making sure there would be someone who would love Kathy, people who would look after her. David's actions guaranteed there would be a family who would care for his wife long after he was gone.

> **We believe that every life has the power to live on in the lives of others, especially when we choose to place the needs of others before our own.**

We believe that every life has the power to live on in the lives of others, especially when we choose to place the needs of others before our own. When this happens, we leave a legacy built on the relationships we possess and known by the love we share.

In the face of her husband's death, Kathy found herself surrounded by family, because David understood that a life of love and compassion lives on long after we breathe our last.

Like the chapters of a book, our lives are bound to come to an end. But we all have the opportunity to let our stories live on in the lives of those we love. The last words written in our book can leave the world a better place.

If today were the day, would you be proud of the moments that brought you here?

What will you leave behind when your ink runs out?

Part Two
Life Is like LEGOs

Just because you're using the same tool doesn't
mean you'll end up with the same result.

– Unknown

OUR LIVES ARE FILLED WITH EXPERIENCES that shape who we are
and who we will one day become. Adventures and struggles leave
marks on us; the way others treat us helps mold us. Some of our
experiences are unique, but as we grow and mature, it becomes
apparent that most of the things we endure in life aren't all that
singular. There is always someone who has walked a similar path.

What truly sets us apart is what we choose to do with our
experiences—the memories, the joys, the pain. Our lives are built
from the collection of pieces we gather through these experiences,
and it's all too easy to put them together in a particular way, never
rearranging them, never examining a piece and wondering if there
is a better place for it, or if we need that piece at all. What pieces of
your life need rearranging? What are you missing? What seemingly
random collection of bricks are lying around you that you can use
to build something amazing?

Look at Me

9

It is only when we are known that we are positioned to become conduits of love. And it is love that transforms our minds, makes forgiveness possible, and weaves a community of disparate people into the tapestry of God's family.

– Curt Thompson

IN THE HEART OF EVERY MAN, WOMAN, AND CHILD is a desire to be seen—to be recognized as important. There is so much beauty in the moments when we are not just acknowledged but our existence is embraced as significant. When someone sees past our fears and failures and looks into our hearts and loves us just because we are human, we are drawn into one of the most powerful human experiences—being known.

This desire to be known is at the center of so much pain, addiction, and depression. The hurt that manifests when we are treated as less than or feel unknown is unlike any other, because it makes us feel as if our connection with humanity has been severed.

We must remember that every person is significant and we have the ability to let others know this; we have countless opportunities to instill this understanding in the people around us through simple acts.

Because often, what seems like the simplest of acts can have the most significant impact.

———

Sometimes you don't realize you're doing something wrong until you see someone else doing it right.

A few years ago, my family and I (Patrick) were spending a long weekend with my friend Ted, his wife Amee, and their two boys in a cabin in Waldport, Oregon. We played in the sand, barbecued, sipped drinks in the hot tub, and played games late into the night.

> **When someone sees past our fears and failures and looks into our hearts and loves us just because we are human, we are drawn into one of the most powerful human experiences— being known.**

The day before we were scheduled to leave, Ted and I decided to go crabbing where the Alsea River and Pacific Ocean meet. The brackish water would be ideal to catch plenty of crab.

Once we had secured our rented boat and loaded it with our crab pots and some soup bones for bait, we were ready to go. Just before we pushed off the dock, we spotted a man who looked to be in his seventies walking toward us. He carried a tackle box in his weathered right hand and a fishing pole in his left. His thick gray whiskers against his sun-kissed skin gave him a rugged look. And on top of his head, he wore a black hat with embroidered gold letters across the front that said, "Vietnam Veteran."

Ted approached the man. "Excuse me, sir."

The man nodded slightly at Ted. "What can I do for you, son?"

Pointing to the man's hat, Ted said, "You're a vet?" It sounded more like a statement than a question.

In a mildly tense tone, the United States war veteran said, "Yes I am."

Ted reached out his hand and said, "Thank you for your service."

The gentleman took Ted's hand in a firm grip, and I could see the faintest of smiles on the man's face as the corner of his mouth curled up ever so slightly. I thought to myself, *Why don't I do that?*

> **Sometimes you don't realize you're doing something wrong until you see someone else doing it right.**

Though their interchange was brief, the gentleman's hard exterior softened as he said, "Thank you, young man. You have no idea what it means to me to hear you say that." He nodded to me. "You boys have fun out there."

We did. The outboard motor on our boat didn't give us the greatest speed, but we found a line where the water pattern was different, signaling to us that this was the deepest part of the mouth of the river. We dropped our five crab pots filled with meat and bone about fifty feet apart, and Ted then piloted the little boat back to our first pot where we grabbed the rope attached to the buoy and pulled the crab trap to the surface as fast as we could so no crabs would escape. After an hour or so, we had more than twenty Dungeness crabs ready to be cooked for dinner.

That evening, the four of us adults sat in the sand, eating fresh crabmeat and drinking white wine, while our five collective children ran through the surf. We talked about the cold weather, the storm clouds in the distance, and how good fresh crab tasted.

As I finished a bite, I said to Ted, "That meant a lot to him; you could see it in his eyes."

It took Ted a second to shift gears from the casual conversation, but after a moment, he nodded. "I make a point to do that any time I come across a vet, a firefighter, a policeman, or a teacher. Those are hard careers, often thankless ones. People need to know we see them."

I can't tell you how many times I have seen Ted do this since, and he encourages his boys to do it as well.

I've learned a lot from Ted. Every time I see someone wearing a uniform or a hat that identifies them as a veteran, I thank them for the work they do and the sacrifices they make, willingly facing danger to keep families like mine safe. And recently, I have been encouraging my kids to do the same.

Just a few months ago, I watched as my ten-year-old son, Joshua, walked up to a man wearing a Korean War Veteran hat. He said, "Excuse me, sir."

The man looked down at him, and Joshua said, "I just want to say thank you for serving our country." As my boy stuck out his hand for the stranger to shake, the man smiled.

"Thank you, young man," the veteran said, tears in his eyes.

He shook hands with the young boy standing in front of him and opened his mouth to say something else, but the quiver of his lips made him hold his words back. Instead, his mouth spread into a huge smile, and a tear dripped down his face. Before he turned to walk away, he patted my son gently on the shoulder and forced out one more, "Thank you."

I will never know what he was about to say to Joshua, but I could tell it meant the world to him that a boy had taken a moment to let him know he was known.

———

There are moments in every single day where we have the opportunity to show someone that they are known, that their existence is acknowledged, and that they are important.

We can do this through getting to know the waitstaff in the

restaurants we frequent, calling them by name, and taking an interest in their days. We can do this by looking a member of the armed forces or a police officer in the eyes and thanking them for the sacrifice they have made to keep our people safe.

Every human being can and should take the time to invest in others the way Ted has. The cascading effects spread into the lives of others as they become both receivers and givers of being known. It's easy to draw lines separating us, outlining whether or not we support a war effort, ascribe to a particular political party, or practice a certain faith. But taking the time for others is unifying; it reminds us that we are all trying to find our way.

> There are moments in every single day where we have the opportunity to show someone that they are known, that their existence is acknowledged, and that they are important.

We have seen friends pass a homeless man on a street corner, walk into a nearby restaurant, and then head back to sit with the man and share a meal, talking about whatever he wants to discuss. We know women who volunteer time at a women's shelter, teaching residents how to cook as they reenter life after spending years in prison. There are people in our community who work with local churches, using their kitchens as places to make meals for the hungry. They look each person in the eyes as they come through the line, asking them their name and thanking them for coming to dinner.

Knowing others looks like children on a playground recognizing the kid no one else wants to play with and asking, "Will you play with us?"

Knowing others looks like counselors and teachers offering the child whose world is turned upside down a safe place to just be.

The classroom or office becomes a shelter where they experience a reprieve from the trauma of their life.

Knowing others looks like taking a minute to get to know the coworker that keeps to herself, learning about her interests.

Knowing others happens in any moment where we take the time to offer others love and compassion.

And when others experience this, they are more inclined to pass this gift on to those they meet—taking a little more time, showing a little more interest, sharing a little bit of life.

The idea of knowing others is at the heart of recovery groups like Alcoholics Anonymous, a place where individuals feel safe sharing what they are dealing with, a place where they can acknowledge the pain their decisions have caused, a place where they are valued regardless of past experiences or choices. This concept is the foundation of support groups for families dealing with ALS as they walk the journey of a loved one facing certain death. The desire to know others and be known by others is fundamental to human existence, and each of us has the power to feed this need.

We never know when our efforts to spend a little time with someone will make a lasting difference in their life. We will never understand the impact of a ten-year-old boy's genuine thanks given to a retired serviceman. But we do know actions like these always leave an imprint. They always fill others up with a sense of love and purpose. They're pieces in the puzzle of life that remind others of their value.

Because sometimes, what seems like the simplest of acts can have the most significant impact.

Unexpected

10

There is frequently more to be learned from the unexpected questions of a child than the discourses of men.

– John Locke

LIFE IS AN AMALGAMATION of the unplanned and the spontaneous, the monotonous and the exciting, things we enjoy and others we would rather not experience. From the careers we pursue to the relationships we cultivate, we all are bound to face every emotion on the spectrum over the course of our lives. The highs and lows of marriage, the joys and pains of parenting, the heartbreak of saying good-bye to loved ones gone too soon—these and many other experiences shape us; they give us the pieces that make us; they are a part of our identity.

The two of us are both fathers, and we have been blessed with some amazing kids and are married to incredible women. But our journeys of fatherhood and marriage aren't always amazing or incredible. Life is filled with work, struggles, moments of compromise, and a whole lot of learning along the way. It is within the collection of life's lessons, pleasant and unpleasant, that we discover who we are and who we should be. Our past life experiences influence our future decisions, help us gain a deeper understanding of the people we encounter, and sometimes offer us much-needed new perspectives. Those experiences often come from unlikely places, like a complete stranger or a friend's child.

> It is within the collection of life's lessons, pleasant and unpleasant, that we discover who we are and who we should be.

Just like life, children are a mixture of the unplanned and spontaneous, offering both the monotonous and the exciting, but rarely in equal parts. They are constantly catching us off guard with untimely filled diapers, surprise spills, unfiltered public comments about strangers' clothing choices or body odor, the new four-letter word they learned on the playground, and moments of startling wisdom. A lesson may be waiting for us in the words they say or the things they do . . . or in the people they meet.

———

Small groups are a common part of many church environments. Different churches call them by different names—life groups, cell groups, or more "creative" names like "Change Makers" or "Soul Squads." But regardless of what you call them, these regular gatherings all operate with the same basic principles—providing a space to discuss life, seek a better understanding of an individual's role in the world, try to understand God and what it means to love others, and offer one another support and accountability through the different stages and trials of life. Some are a mixture of varying age groups—a collection of mentors and mentees—while others are made up of people in the same stage of life, like newlyweds or young parents. The most common challenge for couples with young children is what to do with their kiddos one night a week while they attend small groups. Hiring babysitters on a weekly basis gets expensive!

Marcus and Jill were dealing with this exact situation. With two young children, one still in diapers, they and several other families struggled to meet on a regular basis until one member of their small group offered up their home for the weekly meetings and their bonus room as a place for the children to play while the adults met. Each week, one couple took a turn supervising the group of three- to eight-year-olds while the rest of the parents met downstairs. Though they discussed a variety of topics, the challenges and joys of parenting were the ones most frequently addressed. From discipline styles to bedtime routines to work/home-life balance, the couples explored what others were doing, passed around tips, and offered support.

After a few months of meeting, Jill brought up the topic of service and different ways the group could actively pursue helping others in their community. She wanted to make sure the group did more than talk about the good they could do; she wanted to show their children what it means to love others. Everyone agreed that instilling a desire to serve at an early age was paramount.

Over the course of several years, each family participated in a variety of service projects—feeding the homeless at a local shelter, collecting blankets and clothing for newly arriving refugee families, making sure kids in underserved communities had food and warm coats. The children were always involved, but after a few years together, the parents decided they wanted the kids to do more than be a part of serving; they wanted the children to take the reins.

After the topic was raised, the kids discussed different ideas. Some were as grand as building an orphanage or ending world hunger, but the kiddos finally agreed on something they could dig into right away. They wanted to give valentines to people who might not otherwise receive them. One of the kids' grandparents had recently passed away in a retirement home, so delivering valentines to a group of men and women at the same facility seemed a logical place to start.

When one of the parents asked Jill's daughter, "Why valentines?" the young girl replied, "People need to know they are loved."

The plan was made, and time was set aside. But the kids wanted to do more than simply deliver the valentines; they wanted to make them. For two weeks, rather than the adults meeting as couples, everyone met together as families. Stacks of paper with every color of the rainbow, glue, glitter, stickers, stamps, and scissors populated tables, countertops, and empty space on the kitchen floor.

> **"People need to know they are loved."**

Creations of all kinds came to life as imaginations ran wild. It was amazing to see how many valentines eight kids could make. One of the parents called the retirement home inquiring about the number of residents. Forty-seven men and women lived at the facility. Forty-seven valentines were made.

When the day came to make the delivery, the families all loaded up in their cars and headed to the retirement home. Each child seemed to vibrate with excitement as they talked about sharing what they had made with their soon-to-be friends.

Everyone checked in at the front desk, where the staff was expecting them, and after a quick tour of the common room and dining hall, one of the workers escorted the families into a main hallway. The walls were lined with doors, each one offering admittance to the variety of apartments. A few housed elderly couples, but most were the residences of widows or widowers. Marcus and Jill walked with their daughter and son to one of the apartments, knocked on the open door, and were invited in.

The eyes of a white-haired woman in her late eighties lit up as she said, "Well, what do we have here?"

"Valentines!" both kids announced with joy.

The scene was the same in every room. The residents gratefully received the attention from wide-eyed, innocent boys and girls wanting nothing more than to share their creations of love.

The deliveries continued till just a few rooms remained. Jill and Marcus's daughter walked ahead of them down the corridor with her last valentine in her hands—a red piece of paper with a white heart and the words *Happy Valentine's Day! Someone Loves You!* written in pink marker and covered in glitter. The young girl had become quite comfortable since they had first arrived. Without hesitation, she walked into one of the remaining apartments ahead of her parents without knocking and announced her presence with a loud and excited, "Happy Valentine's Day! This is for you!"

The only person in the room was a gray-haired man sitting in a recliner, reading a newspaper. He turned at the high-pitched declaration and stared at the girl who had entered his room uninvited.

Marcus caught up with his daughter and apologized for the intrusion, but the man waved away the apology. A warm smile spread across his face, and he asked, "And who might you be?"

"I'm your valentine!" the little girl declared, bouncing with too much excitement to contain.

The man chuckled and said, "Is that so?"

The girl nodded.

Eyeing the card in her hands, the man continued, "Well, my valentine, my name is Richard."

"Hi, Richard," said the girl as she held out the valentine. Wrinkled, veiny hands reached out to accept the gift.

Holding the card up, Richard inspected it and said, "Well, this is unexpected. Did you make this?"

The little girl nodded excitedly.

"You know, it has been a long time since I've received a valentine like this," Richard continued. "The people here make sure we're not forgotten, but what you have here is something you've made; this is very different than a card you buy at the store."

Setting the card down in his lap, Richard began tracing the letters with his finger.

"Do you like it?" the girl asked.

Nodding his head but keeping his eyes on the card, Richard said, "I do. I like it very much." He looked up at his new friend and asked, "Do you know who used to make me Valentine's Day cards every year?"

"No."

The smile on Richard's face grew even wider. "My wife. She loved to make little things like this."

Head tilted and eyes squinting, the girl asked, "Why doesn't she anymore?"

"She died a long time ago."

"Oh."

A somber quiet took over the room for a few moments until Richard looked up at Marcus and Jill. He stared Jill in the eyes, unblinking, for a few seconds before turning to Marcus and doing the same.

With a nod of his head he said, "Thank you." Turning back to Jill he continued, "Both of you."

"For what? She made it," Marcus said with a grin.

"Yes, she did. But you are making her into something beautiful. Don't stop doing what you're doing. The world needs unexpected acts of love."

Turning back to the young girl, Richard reached for her hand. Holding her small fingers gently, he smiled and said, "And thank you, my valentine."

———

Defining moments can hit us without warning. Whether they are filled with joy or loss, they give us something to work with—new pieces to our puzzle, new materials with which to build our lives.

Jill and Marcus were gifted one of those defining moments. Because of the desire to give heartfelt gifts, the children in their small group created an opportunity for something unexpected. Simple things like valentines are often not so simple. A little girl's wide-eyed love for others gave Richard a beautiful gift, but Marcus and Jill received something even greater: the wisdom in the words, "The world needs unexpected acts of love."

> **If we choose to not grow up completely, to maintain a little bit of that childhood wonder; if we decide to not conform to society's ideas of love and transactional relationships, people will have the opportunity to experience love that is real, love that is pure.**

Relationships without expectations aren't realistic, and some expectations aren't bad. Our kids expect us to feed them, but this doesn't make our doing so any less loving. However, there is a different kind of power that resides in the unexpected. We are called to love without conditions, without expecting anything in return. A challenging task when we are surrounded by our culture's twisted rules of engagement—give to get and love to be loved. But if we choose to not grow up completely, to maintain a little bit of that childhood wonder; if we decide to not conform to society's ideas of love and transactional relationships, people will have the opportunity to experience love that is real, love that is pure.

We all have something to give—time and money, compassion and grace, love and mercy, or maybe a valentine. Give them freely, without expectation, and you will learn a thing or two along the way.

A Single Moment

11

I don't want to be the center of anything, just a part of something bigger.

– Amber Run (From the song "Pilot")

HUMANITY CAN BE INCREDIBLY SELFISH—and remarkably deceptive. While our self-centered motives are sometimes painfully clear, we often shroud our egocentrism and greed in acts of service, mask our desire for attention as loving gestures, or project false humility because what we really want is martyrdom.

We have all met the people who volunteer at a homeless shelter because they genuinely want to help, and we have witnessed others who do so because they want people to know that they volunteer. If we're honest with ourselves, we have all, at some time, been both the honest volunteer and the look-at-me poser. Greed for attention and recognition is as universal as it is terrible.

There is no denying that our intentions matter. The motivations behind our actions are just as important as the actions themselves, sometimes even more so. Because when we fall into the trap of misaligned motivations and behaviors, we become toxic—mostly to ourselves. We begin to believe that we are more important than the work we are doing or the people we are serving. But if we're lucky, something or someone will open our eyes to a specific truth.

———

As a young physician, Jim Souza was an idealist, ready to save the world one patient at a time. Board certified in critical care medicine and pulmonary disease, he saw patients in his clinic for a variety of respiratory conditions and worked in the intensive care units (ICUs) of several area hospitals in Boise, Idaho. There was no shortage of people who needed the skill and expertise of a critical care physician, and Jim was making an impact.

The motivations behind our actions are just as important as the actions themselves, sometimes even more so.

But as his experience and patient load grew, his career began to take a toll. Long hours and death are part and parcel of working in the ICU environment; for every patient Jim could help, it felt like there was another one he couldn't save. Soon, the days where he made a difference seemed outnumbered by the ones where it felt like nothing he did was enough. As the years passed, Jim's focus changed.

By 2003, Jim's motivation had shifted from a desire to care for people to simply running a successful practice. He was punching the clock, going through the motions. Proud of how productive he was in paying back student loans, Jim was motivated by the pursuit of a bigger salary, and patient care had become merely a vehicle to get what he wanted as opposed to a passion he pursued.

During that same year, Jim was on call for the ICU when a young man was admitted for acute respiratory failure and acute respiratory distress syndrome (ARDS). Jim reviewed the little information the medical team had on the young man from Mexico.

A migrant worker, the patient had found seasonal labor on a farm in central Idaho. During the week prior to his admission, he had been given the task of cleaning out one of the barns. The young man worked in the enclosed space without respiratory protection, cleaning out manure, dirt, and debris. For several hours, he shoveled, swept, and hauled away whatever he found.

During the days that followed, he developed fevers, unrelenting headaches, violent coughing fits, and shortness of breath. By the time he was admitted to the hospital, he was at the point of death and was immediately placed on a respirator to assist his breathing.

Initial evaluation revealed unusual lab findings, ultimately resulting in a diagnosis of hantavirus pulmonary syndrome (HPS).

HPS is a highly lethal disease, caused by exposure to a virus that is shed in the urine, saliva, and droppings of infected deer mice. When areas infested with disease-carrying mice are disturbed, the virus becomes airborne, and people are infected when they inhale the particles floating in the air. With a mortality rate of nearly 50 percent, the disease progresses rapidly from symptoms like fever, chills, nausea, vomiting, and shortness of breath to severe hypotension (low blood pressure) and acute respiratory failure.

In addition to all this, Jim's new patient was in shock, and within hours of admission, many of his organs began to fail.

Though death was the most likely outcome, Jim and the medical staff did everything they could to give the young man his best chance of survival. The virus ran its course, and the patient eventually stabilized. A tracheostomy was placed to allow for long-term ventilator support, but within a few weeks the medical team was able to remove the ventilator, and Jim's patient began to recover.

Today, many hospitals have teams of ICU physicians that share the workload of various patients, but at that time, most hospitals had not yet designed a robust system of care in their ICUs. This meant that if a patient was admitted to Jim on his on-call day, that patient was Jim's until they either died or were discharged.

Fortunately, the patient continued to improve and was eventually transferred out of the ICU to the medical floor, where Jim continued to oversee his care.

As the patient came out of the haze caused by his respiratory failure and the host of necessary medications and treatments, Jim learned through an interpreter that the young man's family all lived in Mexico and there were no local family members to update. Besides the very basic details, Jim never really took the time to learn anything else about the man—something he would regret for the rest of his life. But he was incredibly busy, working more than eighty hours per week, running a medical practice with six other physicians, doing his best to care for his patients, and being a husband and father to three young children.

Jim was working so hard to perform the mechanics of his job that he had lost touch with the human component to the care he provided.

After almost a week on the medical floor, Jim's HPS patient had improved to the point that he was ready for discharge. On the day the young man was set to leave the hospital, Jim walked into his room with an interpreter.

Jim stood at the foot of the bed while the interpreter sat next to the young man, ready to convey his discharge instructions. Jim explained the details of the patient's diagnosis, walked through the gradual recovery that would continue, gave exercise and dietary instructions, described the potential long-term impacts on his respiratory health, and urged him to make a follow-up appointment.

As Jim spoke, the interpreter repeated his words in Spanish, and the young man listened intently. When the patient nodded and told the interpreter he understood, Jim turned to leave the hospital room.

However, before he was out the door, he heard his patient say something in Spanish. Some of the words sounded familiar, but he didn't quite catch them.

"Don't leave," the interpreter said to Jim.

Jim turned to face her with a confused look.

She smiled and said, "He wants to thank you."

Jim nodded and said, "Okay," assuming he would hear "Gracias."

"Move closer," the young woman instructed.

Thinking the patient wanted to speak softly, Jim stepped toward the hospital bed.

The patient turned to the interpreter and said something quietly to her.

She nodded and said to Jim, "No, closer."

Jim took another step so that he was standing next to his patient. The man lying in the hospital bed grabbed both of Jim's hands in his own and pulled them together. Without saying a word, he leaned forward and kissed both of Jim's hands.

Jim just stood there, speechless. You would need to know Jim to understand how unusual this is. This man's simple act of gratitude, in a single moment, reminded Jim of the power that exists in human connection and the beauty of the work he is privileged to do with the gifts and skills God has given him.

Jim has many patient stories—heartbreaking losses, recoveries that border on miraculous—but none of them have had as profound of an effect on him as this one. Jim's recollection is a stark reminder that we should never lose sight of the things that matter most:

> Unfortunately, he never did keep that follow-up
> appointment. I suspect he went back to Mexico, and
> certainly had no resources to keep an appointment
> anyway.

To this day, I regret that I don't recall his name, because if I could, I would find him and thank him. I am eternally grateful for the simple and humble gift of thanks he gave to me. It is one of the most precious patient-care experiences I have had. He woke me back up at a time when I was losing sight of the connections that bind us all.

———

Fortunately, we will never know what kind of path Jim would have gone down if not for a Mexican migrant worker's gift of gratitude. Though the intentions behind Jim's actions had become compromised, a single moment changed everything because another man's intentions were pure.

Scripture is rife with passages about the power, beauty, and necessity of humility. Philippians 2:3-7 paints a vivid picture of what true humility looks like:

> Do nothing out of selfish ambition or vain conceit. Rather, in humility value others above yourselves, not looking to your own interests but each of you to the interests of the others.
>
> In your relationships with one another, have the same mindset as Christ Jesus:
>
> Who, being in very nature God, did not consider equality with God something to be used to his own advantage; rather, he made himself nothing by taking the very nature of a servant, being made in human likeness.

So much power can rest in a single moment. Because he chose a position of pure humility and gratitude, a young patient offered the course correction Jim so desperately needed. In a single moment, he helped Jim rediscover the passion behind the career he had chosen and the love he has for the people he serves.

The beauty that hangs in the balance of life and death is powerful, but it is no more important than the wonder and joy available to all of us in our daily interactions with family, friends, and strangers.

> "In your relationships with one another, have the same mindset as Christ Jesus."

We may not always recognize it, but we are surrounded by people who live with humility, people who are grateful for who we are and what we do. May we have eyes to see them, hearts to know them, and a willingness to embrace their gifts so we can stay on the right path—so that we can someday offer the same thing to someone else.

Never underestimate the power of a single moment.

Five Little Words

12

We cannot seek achievement for ourselves and forget about progress and prosperity for our community. . . . Our ambitions must be broad enough to include the aspirations and needs of others, for their sakes and for our own.

– Cesar Chavez

THE WORD *HEALTHY* is an adjective used for many different things— objects, activities, organizations. Simply defined as nourishing, wholesome, or beneficial, healthy can describe food, exercise, businesses, churches, and communities.

Foods identified as healthy provide us with essential vitamins, minerals, and calories, nutrients we can use to fuel our bodies. Healthy exercises promote strength, flexibility, or endurance, while not putting joints and muscles at risk for injury—they benefit the body. A healthy business benefits owners and employees alike because retention is high, work/life balance is encouraged, and margins are heading in the right direction. When a church is healthy, people support one another, service is a priority, and relationships are cultivated.

But health doesn't come easy. To eat in a way that benefits the body requires planning, education, and knowledge. Exercise is work in and of itself, not to mention the time we must set aside to do it.

Achieving health takes work—especially when it comes to relationships. Any time two or more people are involved in anything—businesses, churches, nonprofits, marriages, friendships, parenting—health is the result of a monumental amount of effort.

We say things like, "They have such a healthy marriage" or "Her relationships with her kids are amazing" and jump to the conclusion that life is just easier for those folks. It's not. Healthy relationships are filled with sacrifice. But such relationships are the heartbeat of anything we do that is worthwhile.

However, creating healthy relationships is becoming more and more difficult as society pushes egocentric agendas and social media connects us without really connecting us. So how do we dig in and build friendships that last? How do we cultivate relationships at home and in the workplace that allow each of us to be everything we can be for one another?

> Achieving health takes work—especially when it comes to relationships.

We believe the answer is found in five little words—*honesty, vulnerability, accountability, intentionality,* and *community.* But before we can embrace what these five words can do for us, we need to understand what they truly mean.

We understand every relationship has remarkable potential and any shared accomplishment is extraordinary because of the communication and level of connection it requires. Ultimately, the ability of an individual to move through life is dependent upon the degree to which they engage in their relationships.

Not a day goes by that we don't see young men and women sitting across from each other, enthralled in Twitter, Instagram, Facebook, or Snapchat, or texting with someone else as opposed to looking the person across from them in the eye and partaking in honest and real conversation. The things missing here are the very things close relationships require to thrive—honesty, vulnerability, accountability, intentionality, and community.

These elements of relationship are deeply connected. But each plays a specific part in creating a healthy dynamic.

What does it mean to be honest? The modern definition of this word is "to be genuine, truthful, sincere, and honorable in one's principles." This is where many people lose their honesty and don't even know it. The word's origin (the Latin word *honos*) means to be held in or deserving of honor.

Our society often uses *truthful* and *honest* interchangeably. But if we only embrace the "truthful" portion of the definition, we can get ourselves in some major trouble. How many times have you heard someone protest, "I'm just being honest!" when they say something that is true but intended to hurt someone else or cause conflict? Have you ever been guilty of offering up factual information—truthful information—with the intent of stirring the pot? Being truthful and being honest are not mutually inclusive.

There are times in every relationship when we might tell ourselves we're being honest with a friend or partner, but our motives don't line up. No matter how true our words might be, if they are said with the intent to wound, our behavior is not honorable, and therefore we are not being honest.

Saying one thing and meaning another is not honest. Passive-aggressive communication is not honest. Using words as weapons (no matter how true they are) is not honest.

When we embrace true honesty, making it a fundamental ingredient in our relationships, others will come to know they can trust that what we say is true, *and* we have their best interests in mind. This kind of honesty creates a safe place where we can be vulnerable without fear.

———

A few years ago, Justin and I (Patrick) were wrapping up a day of speaking with a dinner party. Holding my glass of wine in my left hand, I raised Justin's to his lips with my right. We had delivered a keynote earlier in the day about the power of human connection and were now enjoying conversation with fellow speakers, sponsors, and conference attendees.

A tall, broad-shouldered man in a gray suit approached us, salt-and-pepper hair combed back, eyes narrow behind round glasses. We recognized him from earlier, when he had delivered an eloquent, thoughtful talk on community health.

He sized us up and then blurted out with an air of disgust, "When I first saw you guys, I knew you were full of [crap]!"

Justin and I just looked at him. The air was suddenly tainted with a cloud of awkwardness. *Is this guy for real?*

Then he smiled. "I'm glad to know I was wrong!" He then asked how two men could have such a deep, raw, and intimate connection. "I want what you guys have; I just don't know how to do it."

I smiled. "I can't speak for Justin, but I know what our lifelong relationship has required of me. Complete honesty about my fears and failures, full disclosure of my temptations, and a willingness to lay down the burdens I carry so he can pick them up for me. Complete vulnerability."

The man's narrow eyes were replaced with wide saucers. "The thought of being that open with another person, let alone another man, is terrifying!"

———

This interaction sums up how so many people feel about vulnerability. Being vulnerable is often associated with weakness, and showing others our weaknesses is countercultural—for some, even counterintuitive. Fear is often our first reaction when we are challenged to shed some skin. We fear rejection, being considered unworthy. This trepidation is made even more powerful when we have histories of trauma or abuse. Circumstances and life experiences often give us reason to not trust others. But any healthy relationship is grounded in love and acceptance, loving each other regardless of how worthy or unworthy we might be. There is beauty on the other side of vulnerability.

Not too long ago, as we sat with some friends, we discussed what being vulnerable looks like. Their insights were profound. One of them stated, "Only when someone knows all of me can they truly love me."

Only when someone knows all of me can they truly love me.

Being vulnerable is a terrifying prospect, but these words are so true. And this idea is the foundation of any close relationship.

There isn't a thing the two of us don't know about one another—each fear, every failure, and all of the skeletons in the closet. It turns out that a healthy friendship isn't much different than a healthy marriage. No secrets, and for better or for worse.

> **Any healthy relationship is grounded in love and acceptance, loving each other regardless of how worthy or unworthy we might be.**

When we trust others with all of who we are, we give them the opportunity to love all of who we are. Sharing just the good stuff—the things we are proud of, the things that don't scare us—makes for pretty shallow relationships. But when someone chooses to love us because and in spite of who we are—that's real love. It's the closest thing to unconditional love we will experience. A kind of magic happens when we lay everything on the table.

When practiced together, honesty and vulnerability create a unique dynamic. The level of honesty and vulnerability we embrace determines the level of accountability we can have with one another.

Life is a journey, and we never arrive! No matter how hard we work, how much we study, or how hard we train, there is always a better version of ourselves out there waiting for us. The second we think we have arrived, that better version of us becomes more distant. And if we continue to swallow the lie, our better self will elude us forever.

But when we pursue honesty and vulnerability in relationships, something beautiful is able to thrive. Something that keeps each of us from thinking we have arrived. Something that lets us discover the better version of ourselves waiting beyond each new experience. The us our friends deserve, the us our spouses deserve, the us our children deserve. That something beautiful is accountability.

But let's be *honest*—embracing accountability is scary. It means we have to face that we're fallible, we're going to be wrong, we don't have some things figured out, we're not perfect. To make matters even more terrifying, being accountable means letting others know all about our dark, yucky stuff—the dirt. It means not only allowing others to see the painful struggles we face, but also being okay with them calling us out on the behaviors that make us less than we can be, the behaviors keeping us from attaining a better version of who we are.

There are many reasons people live on the surface, never really sharing all they are—never being vulnerable and honest, let alone accountable. If we are *truthful* with ourselves, we all have been there at some point: walking through life wearing masks, hoping no one sees through them. Pretending we have arrived but knowing deep down we are slaves to identities built on secrets, lies, and omissions of truth. Who wants to live like that?

Accountability is so freeing. Pursuing relationships with honesty and vulnerability allows our loved ones to know and love all of us. And when we give them permission to hold us accountable, our fears, addictions, and secrets have less power. Rather than being slaves to our weaknesses, we are free of them. This doesn't mean we never fail or fall back into old habits, but it does mean we have people who will pick us up or correct our compasses so we can get back on course. Rather than being concerned with whether or not someone can see behind the masks we wear, we begin to shift our focus toward who we can become.

We've said it before, building healthy relationships takes work! There is no easy-to-follow recipe—no magic sauce. If deep, meaningful relationships were natural, we would see a lot more of them. But we don't because we live in a world where we believe things should come easy, so when relationships get hard, our society often looks for the easy way out instead of pursuing them with intentionality.

The word *relationship* simply refers to how two or more things are connected. When two people work together, they have a relationship in the context of work. When two kids live next door, they have a relationship in the context of being neighbors. And when two people share similar interests, goals, and outlooks on life, and spend time together, they have a relationship or friendship based on those interests they share.

Often relationships, both romantic and platonic, begin because of these common interests, but they will only carry a relationship so far. Combine those interests with intentionality, and watch out!

Whether in a marriage or friendship, our shared interests, our shared experiences, and our shared memories create threads of connection that bind us together. But if we aren't careful, the busyness of life can distract us. And when we become distracted, the frequency and depth of our shared experiences lessen, our shared memories become distant, and the threads that hold us together become strained, fray, and, if we aren't careful, break.

This is where intentionality comes in. Intentionality refers to being *deliberate* or *purposeful*—deliberately spending time with loved ones, purposefully placing their needs above your own. This takes work and focus, but the payoff is incredible. When a relationship is grounded in *honesty*, *vulnerability*, and *accountability*, *intentionality* is a little easier to pursue.

The two of us have a friendship in which we share similar tastes in music, similar political views, and the same stupid sense of humor. But what gives depth and breadth to our relationship are the memories we have intentionally made, the adventures we have intentionally pursued, the time we have intentionally spent. Being deliberate and purposeful is why our friendship has survived and thrived as long as it has.

Our shared interests have made a basic connection possible, but those connections are just threads. The *honesty*, *vulnerability*, and *accountability* we have cultivated over many years make *intentionally* spending time together easier. Each memory we have made because we both make the other a priority, each adventure and shared experience we take on because we intentionally pursue one another, weaves together with those foundational threads of connection, creating ropes that tie us together. The more we live intentionally with one another, the thicker those ropes become. And when the busyness of life does come along, there is little, if anything, that can cause those ropes to become strained or frayed.

How does living intentionally look? What does it mean in the day-to-day? It means we have to pick up the phone and make a call, go to coffee, plan a trip and take it, or show up on the doorstep ready for conversation. Intentionality means enjoying a night out, an afternoon on the back patio, or a walk through the neighborhood. Living with intention means spending time together week in and week out, month in and month out, year in and year out. Intentionality means we must deliberately and purposefully pursue one another.

If we want healthy relationships, then we must intentionally pursue the things that make relationships healthy. We must purposefully live life together.

While having a one-on-one relationship built on these elements is incredible, creating a *community* of friends through the same concepts leads to an even greater beauty. While this often doesn't feel like what church is, this is what church should be. Not the walls of the building in which we gather, but the people we live life with through raw, deep connections.

Any meaningful friendship provides individuals with extraordinary love and support. But there is danger in having only one such relationship. Whether it's a spouse, a significant other, or a friend, one of the worst things we can do to a relationship is expect the other person to meet all our needs or convince ourselves we can meet all of theirs.

The adage "Don't put all your eggs in one basket" definitely applies to relationships. One of the greatest gifts we can give to those we hold dear is cultivating strong bonds with multiple individuals. This creates a healthy community where many intimate relationships can flourish. After all, Jesus had twelve disciples, not just one!

Each person in our lives possesses wisdom, experience, and perspective that differ from our own. They each have strengths and weaknesses—different things to offer. A friend has something a spouse can't give, or a spouse has something that no friend can deliver. No one person can offer everything all the time. To expect this is remarkably unfair because it sets up our friends or our spouses for guaranteed failure. Everything, all the time, is an impossible standard for any human to meet.

Every Monday night we meet with a group of couples on the patio of one of our homes. We laugh, break bread, share life's joys, and partner in life's struggles. Each relationship on that patio is the result of varying degrees of honesty, vulnerability, accountability, and intentionality, leading us to this community—the lifeblood of so much of what we do. These men and women support us; they love us, they pray for us, they carry our burdens for us, they are there whenever we need them. Together, our joys are multiplied, and our pains are divided. It's through these types of relationships that we get to experience God's love for us, his provision for us. Through these relationships, he provides us with love, joy, strength, and support. Through this community, he draws us closer to himself.

> **God created us all to live in relationship with him, and often that relationship is experienced as we engage in life with one another.**

God created us all to live in relationship with him, and often that relationship is experienced as we engage in life with one another.

We were never meant to live in solitude. We were created to live in community with one another so we can know love and so we don't have to navigate the struggles of life on our own. Any relationship grounded in honesty, vulnerability, accountability, and intentionality is beautiful, but when a group of people living life together embraces the same principles, each person becomes capable of so much more.

More strength.

More faith.

More love.

The Power of the Collective

13

Individual commitment to a group effort—that is what makes a team work, a company work, a society work, a civilization work.

– Vince Lombardi

FOR MANY, SPORTS HOLD LIFE LESSONS. Any decent coach knows that his success depends on the collective talent and dedication of the individual members of his team. One of the greatest NFL coaches in the history of the game knew this better than most. Vince Lombardi not only understood that the success of his team required the contribution of each member, but he also recognized that the power of the collective is the key to success in everything from family to business, and from culture to government. Others are catching on.

There is a growing trend of collaboration between socially minded businesses, philanthropists, governments, and nonprofit organizations who want to remedy complex social issues, like addressing the global problem of malnutrition or starting a statewide initiative to reduce teen substance abuse. When multiple parties with a variety of resources come together in an effort to achieve large-scale and lasting change, the results can be incredible. This trend is known as *collective impact,* and we often see such collaborations effecting change by bringing health and nutrition resources to underserved communities, addressing drug use in inner-city neighborhoods, creating access to clean water in areas decimated by waterborne diseases, or providing counseling resources for the mentally ill.

> **When multiple parties with a variety of resources come together in an effort to achieve large-scale and lasting change, the results can be incredible.**

While the idea of bringing seemingly disparate groups together to address widespread social needs is gaining popularity, the concept is nothing new. We have all seen the effects of such an approach to challenging situations throughout history. It turns out coach Lombardi was spot on.

In recent history, an incredible example of collective impact is the response to the aftermath of Hurricane Harvey in Southern Texas. A category 4 hurricane, Harvey made landfall in Texas on August 25, 2017. With winds of 130 miles an hour and torrential rains, the massive storm threatened the lives of millions of residents. Homes were destroyed, power was lost, access to fresh water was limited, and many lives were cut short. Harvey caused more than $125 billion in damage. Entire neighborhoods were reduced to ruins, schools and childcare centers were left in disarray, and massive flooding prevented many from accessing much-needed health care.

In the wake of this disaster, people responded in an incredible way. Churches and organizations around the country loaded trucks with clean water, diapers, medical supplies, and clothing and sent those trucks to the affected areas. Relief groups like World Hope

International, the Children's Hunger Fund, and World Vision, among many others, provided funds, resources, and manpower to ease the suffering of victims. Temporary medical stations were erected, and hospital staff worked around the clock to make sure those affected received the care they needed.

But perhaps the most notable story to come out of this disaster is that of the Justin J. Watt Foundation. J. J. Watt is known as an incredible defensive end for the Houston Texans, and his strength and athleticism have helped him become recognized as one of the most formidable defensive players in the NFL. But he isn't just known as a professional athlete; Watt is a philanthropist in a league all his own. His foundation, formed in 2010, is driven by the mission of giving children the opportunity to participate in after-school sports programs within a safe environment. But as Hurricane Harvey wreaked havoc on the residents of southeastern Texas, the organization saw a need of a different kind.

In response to the devastation, J. J. Watt rallied the troops to bring hope and resources to the people affected by the storm's destruction. Through the efforts of his fans, a myriad of organizations, and his own resources, more than $41 million in relief was raised and distributed. Those funds were used to repair and rebuild homes, restore childcare centers, give meals to millions, distribute medication to people in desperate need, and provide health care to those going without.

When a collection of individuals allow their passions, talents, and resources to merge, we find the human race is at its finest. The whole is greater than the sum of its parts.

The work of the Justin J. Watt Foundation is just one example among many where people have come together to meet the needs of so many who are suffering—acts of compassion made possible by the hands of many working together for one common objective.

Humanity is remarkable. Each person has the capacity to do great things; bring two people together in a healthy working relationship, friendship, or marriage, and there is incredible potential for energy, love, and compassion to flourish. But when a collection of individuals allow their passions, talents, and resources to merge, we find the human race is at its finest. The whole is greater than the sum of its parts.

But collective impact isn't limited to addressing social epidemics or disasters. This concept of coming together to achieve more than we can on our own can and should be a part of our everyday lives. A biblical story in the book of Luke beautifully illustrates the power of what we can do to help others when we come together around a common goal.

> While Jesus was teaching, some proud religious law-
> keepers and teachers of the Law were sitting by Him. They
> had come from every town in the countries of Galilee
> and Judea and from Jerusalem. The power of the Lord
> was there to heal them. Some men took a man who was
> not able to move his body to Jesus. He was carried on a
> bed. They looked for a way to take the man into the house
> where Jesus was. But they could not find a way to take
> him in because of so many people. They made a hole in
> the roof over where Jesus stood. Then they let the bed
> with the sick man on it down before Jesus. When Jesus
> saw their faith, He said to the man, "Friend, your sins are
> forgiven."
>
> The teachers of the Law and the proud religious law-
> keepers thought to themselves, "Who is this Man Who
> speaks as if He is God? Who can forgive sins but God

only?" Jesus knew what they were thinking. He said to
them, "Why do you think this way in your hearts? Which
is easier to say, 'Your sins are forgiven,' or, 'Get up and
walk'?

"So that you may know the Son of Man has the right
and the power on earth to forgive sins," He said to the
man who could not move his body, "I say to you, get up.
Take your bed and go to your home." At once the sick
man got up in front of them. He took his bed and went to
his home thanking God. All those who were there were
surprised and gave thanks to God, saying, "We have seen
very special things today."

LUKE 5:17-26, NLV

There are a host of lessons within this Scripture, lessons about
the power God has to forgive and heal, lessons about the ills of
religion trumping relationship, but the one that we take from this
passage is one of community, one of collective impact.

Because of the desire and energy of a group of men, a man who
couldn't walk was able to experience something that would have
been entirely out of reach had he been left to his own devices.
Others saw his need and chose to be the man's hands and feet.

We are all the man on the bed, needing others to carry us;
and we all can be the men who tore a hole in the ceiling, looking
for ways to ease the suffering of a friend. We are all victims of
disaster—and we can all be the J. J. Watts of the world. We possess
power, influence, and resources others need to make it through the
day. But we often don't realize it.

Every one of us has a cross to bear; we all have burdens—
addictions, regrets, fears, and insecurities. And if we aren't careful, these burdens become stones we carry, weighing us down.
And when our hands are filled with these burdens, we are prone to

isolation. Our struggles alienate us from others, blinding us to our potential to show love, compassion, and grace.

But when we enter into relationship and willingly pursue time with others, we begin to see we aren't alone in our struggles. When we partner with others, we become aware of the giftings and strengths they possess. Our collective talents and dedication to each other help us face whatever life throws at us. Soon we find our community is a place where our burdens are set aside, lightening the load we carry. Sometimes we see that we need to let things go, other times it takes someone else reaching out and taking the load from our hands.

> **When we enter into relationship and willingly pursue time with others, we begin to see we aren't alone in our struggles.**

—

Albert Schweitzer was one of the most famous missionaries of the modern era. Schweitzer possessed PhDs in theology and philosophy, and was an accomplished concert organist. In spite of this, he left behind both academic and musical careers so he could set up a medical clinic in French Equatorial Africa. When he was eighty-five years old, Schweitzer was visited by Andrew Davison of Colgate Rochester Seminary. Davison tells how one morning, at around eleven o'clock, he, Schweitzer, and some others were walking up a hill near the medical clinic. The weather was extremely hot, and no shade was to be found anywhere on the hill. Without warning, the eighty-five-year-old Dr. Schweitzer turned and walked away from the group. They watched as he made his way toward an African woman struggling up the hill with a large load of wood for the cook fires. Schweitzer took the entire load of wood from the woman and carried it up the hill for her.

When Schweitzer rejoined the group, one of them asked why he did things like that. Along with the rest of the group, this person was concerned that a man of Dr. Schweitzer's age could get injured doing such things. Dr. Schweitzer looked at the group, then pointed to the woman and said, "No one should ever have to carry a burden like that alone."

———

We were never meant to carry the burdens of life alone—something magical happens when we realize this. As we set our struggles aside, even for a moment, our hands are free to pick up the burdens of another. This is when the true power of a community is realized. As we let others carry what we were never meant to carry on our own, we can turn to someone else who is struggling and lift their burden from their hands, freeing them up to do the same.

> As we set our struggles aside, even for a moment, our hands are free to pick up the burdens of another.

Perhaps the late Coretta Scott King said it best, "The greatness of a community is most accurately measured by the compassionate actions of its members."

When community is fostered, and we place the needs of others above our own, we become an army of people ready to jump in and help others through the death of a loved one, a painful divorce, and every other disaster that awaits. United, the challenges of parenthood, job changes, and financial struggles aren't nearly as challenging, because together, we can always do more and do it better.

Opened Eyes

14

Empathy begins with understanding life from another person's perspective. Nobody has an objective experience of reality. It's all through our own individual prisms.

– Sterling K. Brown

IN OUR FAST-PACED CULTURE, we can meet a variety of people on any given day. Whether we're riding a bus to work, stopping for coffee after dropping the kids off at school, or spending the day in airports, each week we all meet people previously unknown to us. Every day offers us new relationships.

Within these new connections, we sometimes find ourselves talking about shared ideas in faith and politics, and other times we get to see things differently as we view the world through someone else's eyes. Every person we encounter is a wellspring filled with new possibilities—new ideas, new stories, new perspectives.

Some days, we take the time to listen to someone else's viewpoint, seeking to understand their outlook and digest their perceptions. These are the days when we are at our finest, when compassion and love are at the forefront of who we are, when we learn and grow because of what others have to offer.

But then there are the days when we don't appreciate other points of view. Rather than listen to someone we disagree with, we tune them out and devalue their existence, giving them reason to question our integrity and the condition of our hearts. Our lack of appreciation for the perspective of others happens because we fail to recognize how much influence someone's life experience has on the shaping of who they become, or we choose not to care.

Every person we encounter is a wellspring filled with new possibilities—new ideas, new stories, new perspectives.

While this undoubtedly happens with strangers, those closest to us experience this most often. Spouses, close friends, parents, siblings, and children frequently bear the brunt of misunderstandings and frustrations born out of disagreements that could often be avoided—if we would just take a breath and seek to understand where they are coming from, desiring to know why they feel the way they feel.

———

Some of the best conversations I (Patrick) have with my kids occur on car rides to campsites, on backpacking trips, or wrestling in the yard. I like to think that nature has a way of bringing us together; whether on vacation in the mountains or playing outside after school, we seem to connect the most when we are outdoors. But I believe the real magic happens because I'm not distracted: my kids are my only focus in those moments. And when that happens, kids can teach their parents some incredible things.

Recently my son, Joshua, took an interest in snowboarding. My wife and I gave him a new board for his birthday, and we had spent several Saturdays up on the ski hill. I used to snowboard, but three knee surgeries and no more cartilage in my right knee mean I now watch and coach from below. Sometimes we go as a family; other times I'll just take Josh and his younger sister, Olivia, who likes to ski. But on one particular Saturday morning, Josh and I headed up the mountain, just the two of us.

On the drive up we listened to music and talked about Josh's week at school. The fourth grade is filled with great stories—the goofy things Josh and his friends do on the playground, experiments or science projects that far exceed my expectations for a fourth-grade classroom. This kid loves school, is a bit of a thinker, and, like his sisters, he teaches me some of my most needed lessons.

When we arrived, the sky was bright blue, the air was a warm 37 degrees, and the ski hill was busy with athletes of all ages and skill levels. For four hours, Josh rode the lift and worked to perfect his turns.

Later in the day, we enjoyed our lunch by the fire pit, talked with friends, and eventually packed up to head down the hill. Josh sat in the back seat as I carefully navigated the slick roads and sharp corners.

Have you ever had a moment when you were just trucking along, enjoying the simple pleasures of the day, and something came out of the blue and smacked you in the face? It hit you so hard, you had to take a moment to understand what just happened.

Josh and I were listening to music again as we headed down the hill, and a few lines from a song caught my ear.

I'm tired
Of tending to this fire
I've used up all I've collected
I have singed my hands[1]

---

[1] Twenty One Pilots, "Leave the City."

I asked my son, "What do you think the singer is saying here? What is he talking about?"

Josh sat quietly in the back seat, thinking about the question. His answer was a little heavier than I expected. "I think he is saying, 'Sometimes you're just done.' When life gets hard, it's hard to keep going.'"

I don't know why I asked my next question. I didn't really think about it—it just came out. Looking at Josh in the rearview mirror, I asked, "Have you ever felt this way?"

The back seat was unusually quiet for a few seconds. I kept glancing at Josh while keeping my attention on the road. His head was down, slowly nodding as he processed his response. "Yeah."

Josh is ten.

"When?" I asked.

Without missing a beat, he said, "When I was little, and I would get in trouble with you or mom for something, sometimes I wondered if you still loved me." He paused for a few seconds and then continued, "When I felt like that, I wanted to disappear."

A little choked up, I responded, "Even though we've always told you there is nothing you could do to change our love for you?"

"Yeah, because when I was little, I didn't know it yet."

My heart broke for a moment. I asked, "How about now that you're older?"

"No, now I know you love me no matter what."

I have spent a lot of time digesting that conversation. A three- or four-year-old heart and mind process things much differently than those of a ten-year-old. But juxtapose my son's four-year-old heart and mind from six years prior against my then-thirty-seven-year-old ones, and things suddenly get very eye opening. There's a lot I have taken for granted when dealing with conflict, discipline, and instruction. More often than not, I have approached situations with my children from my perspective. Not because I am trying to place more importance on mine than theirs, but because it's easier, it takes less work.

Perspective matters. Sometimes it matters more than anything else. My son's insight has taken me back to the times I have had to discipline my kids. I know I approached those situations with my life experiences; my understanding of love; my perspective of forgiveness, responsibility, and accountability. But my children had only three, four, or five years of experience to shape their view of the world. There was a stark difference between their perspectives and mine. And because I failed to recognize this, I have given each of them moments of doubt.

My youngest daughter, Olivia, joined our family through adoption, but I don't think of her as any different from my other kids. She's blood. But this is my perspective. While I see her as completing our family, her joining us was a process filled with unsettled feelings and the unknown. Her first years of life were very different than mine, and her understanding of connection, separation, fear, and loneliness is something I can only try to comprehend. Olivia will never see the world the same way I do. But her unique perspectives are something I should embrace; they

> **Perspective matters. Sometimes it matters more than anything else.**

are lenses I should do my best to look through whenever she is asking hard questions, challenging authority, or feeling down.

The same goes for my older daughter, Cambria. I will never know what it's like to be a fourteen-year-old girl, and every time I try to "understand" what she is going through without accounting for the differences between her story and mine, I do her a disservice. Her perception of the world matters, but if I'm not careful, I will teach her that it doesn't. She thinks differently, feels differently, and processes the world differently. One of the greatest gifts

I can give Cambria is to allow her perspectives to shape mine just as mine will help shape hers.

————

We believe that our children give us many of our greatest gifts. While being a parent is beautiful in and of itself, our children's innocent and inquisitive minds can call us into amazing depths. Their understanding of the world often exceeds our own. They have so much to offer us, but only if we shut up and listen, and take the time to understand them. They can open our eyes to new and wonderful things, but only if we choose to see them, only if we choose to experience the world through their eyes.

In his book *The 7 Habits of Highly Effective People*, Dr. Stephen R. Covey writes, "Most people do not listen with the intent to understand; they listen with the intent to reply." An expert in the field of interpersonal relations, Covey states that the single most important thing we can do for others is to "Seek first to understand, then to be understood."

There are thousands of sayings addressing the importance of listening and understanding. One of our favorites is the proverb "A fool takes no pleasure in understanding, but only in expressing his opinion" (Proverbs 18:2, ESV).

When we listen with a sincere desire to know someone's perspective, when we seek to understand the heart behind their ideas, beliefs, fears, and aspirations, we are participating in a remarkable act of compassion. We are showing them they are valued, we are demonstrating our love for them, and we are acknowledging they have something to offer us. In moments like these we are showing others they have purpose. And often, our eyes are opened to things we've never seen, our hearts are exposed to things we've never felt, and our minds are filled with things we've never known.

But when we choose the fool's path and "listen with the intent to reply," we are tearing down the person on the other end of the conversation. We are saying their ideas, beliefs, and feelings don't matter. Worse yet, we are declaring that *they* don't matter.

How often do we listen to our kids with the intent to reply, with the drive to fix whatever is wrong, as opposed to listening to their words, their emotions, their hearts? If we want to love our children completely, then we must know them completely—or at least try to. This begins with recognizing that they perceive the world differently than we do. And it continues as we seek to understand the world they see.

When we listen with a sincere desire to know someone's perspective, when we seek to understand the heart behind their ideas, beliefs, fears, and aspirations, we are participating in a remarkable act of compassion.

It turns out the same rules apply to people our own age or older than us. The adults we encounter may have far more life experience than a four-year-old, but their experience and understanding will differ from our own. No one, not a single person, will have the same perspective as we do. Whether we're disciplining a child, having a hard conversation with a husband or wife, or dealing with the difficulties that arise from working with people, we must remember that no one sees things the exact same way we do.

As parents, spouses, and friends, we can't help but wonder how many broken hearts and wounded souls could be avoided if we all would seek to understand someone else's perspective before we react, before we speak, before we expect them to understand our own.

Rally to a Standard

15

Justice has nothing to do with victor nations and vanquished nations, but must be a moral standard that all the world's peoples can agree to. To seek this and to achieve it—that is true civilization.

– Hideki Tojo

BODIES LAY EVERYWHERE—some friends, others foes, but all of them dead from days of war—war over territory, war over beliefs, war fought in the name of distant gods. The stench of stale blood filled the air as the clang of sword striking shield echoed all around. Men continued to fall as the battle raged on. Feeling outnumbered and wondering if they would soon be overrun, the soldiers heard a familiar cry rise above the sounds of battle, one they had etched into their hearts and souls, a cry that meant only one thing—they had to move.

Each soldier turned to see his army's flag held high, anchored to a staff. They couldn't see him, but they knew a fellow soldier stood with that pole in his hands, waving it to capture the attention of his surviving comrades. That simple cloth on a stick was the army's *standard*—a rallying point to bring all soldiers together, a place to unify the remaining forces; and the cry they heard meant every one of them was needed there now.

In ancient times, this was a normal scene for soldiers. As men fought to expand their rulers' territories and take control of resources, conflict was commonplace. Rallying to a standard was a way to survive; it provided each soldier with his greatest chance to live and fight another day.

Today, the word *standard* has a much different meaning. When a business or organization sets standards for the behavior of its employees or for how it wants to impact its clients or the world around it, it expresses the beliefs by which it chooses to operate, demonstrating what it holds dear. Churches do the same thing when writing doctrinal standards or publishing codes of conduct. But when we fix our eyes on the wrong standard, one set up to make ourselves look better or to give us the satisfaction of dehumanizing people we disagree with, the results are disastrous. Thinking about modern-day standards in the context of war offers us some challenging perspectives.

War has been a part of humanity's story since the beginning of time. Often, differing political views, conflicting ideas about human worth, and opposing ideologies rest at its center. Religion and politics have caused more division and sparked more conflict than any other two things since man drew his first breath. But religion holds the darkest history because so much pain has been carried out in the name of love.

———

For millennia, the Bible has been used to justify the murder of millions. Situations where Scripture was taken out of context and used to condone terrible human behaviors plague our history. In the days of American slavery, people used Scripture to support the ownership of other humans. Men have used Bible verses to rationalize the subjugation of women and abuse of children, white supremacists have twisted Scripture to give credence to their evil rhetoric, and hate crimes against LGBTQ people have been called "God's judgment" by the far right. The list continues with the bloody Crusades, the Spanish Inquisition, the mass murder of Native Americans, and genocide in Rwanda. So many atrocities have been and continue to be carried out because "the Bible tells me so."

> **When we fix our eyes on the wrong standard, one set up to make ourselves look better or give us the satisfaction of dehumanizing people we disagree with, the results are disastrous.**

With the power of social media, news feeds in our inboxes, and instantaneous communication with people thousands of miles away, we are more aware of evil than ever before, and yet so many still act in ways that spread pathogens of hate, corruption, and deceit—all in the name of a loving God. This epidemic is as strong now as ever.

It's heartbreaking—all of it. Any act that inflicts pain, fear, or misery on another human being is tragic, and no follower of a loving God, no one who believes in the life, love, and words of Jesus, should defend such behaviors. And yet many of us claiming to be Christians find ourselves doing just that.

We need to rally to a different standard, one Jesus outlined in crystal-clear fashion, leaving no room for misinterpretation. Every act done in the name of God where physical or emotional pain is utilized as a tool, fear is perpetuated, or hate is justified is not God-breathed, regardless of the Scripture quoted. Jesus made this very clear in a few short sentences when a Pharisee tested his understanding of Scripture. The words Jesus used in Matthew 22 completely turned the religious world upside down.

"Teacher, which is the greatest commandment in the Law?"

Jesus replied: "'Love the Lord your God with all your heart and with all your soul and with all your mind.' This is the first and greatest commandment. And the second is like it: 'Love your neighbor as yourself.'"

MATTHEW 22:36-39

The two greatest commandments, according to Jesus, are simple!

Love God!
Love others!

That's it . . .
Or is it?

These are wonderful words to live by, but to stop reading this passage here would do a disservice to the intention of Jesus' words.

In verse 40, he continues, "All the Law and the Prophets hang on these two commandments."

This is a statement of profound importance and yet it is often overlooked. Many theological experts point to this passage as referencing all the teachings of the Bible.

All—not some. This includes the ones we use to make us feel okay about judging our neighbor, the ones we use to make ourselves feel better about our hate-filled rhetoric toward other religions or people who live their lives differently than we do. This includes the Scripture verses used to defend the horrors of immigrant separation, torture, misogyny, homophobia, racism, and the host of other deplorable behaviors that plague the past and present of the Christian church. And this includes the ones we use to justify our contempt for those we consider backwards, intolerant, and hate-filled.

Jesus is giving the Pharisees and every reader of the Scriptures the single most important standard by which to live—the only rallying point that can effectively press back against the darkness.

By Jesus' standard, every passage, every teaching, every prophet, and every law should be examined and applied through the lens of loving God and loving others.

So for a church to follow Jesus means that every piece of Scripture, every story, every verse must be viewed through his words: "'Love the Lord your God with all your heart and with all your soul and with all your mind.' This is the first and greatest commandment. And the second is like it: 'Love your neighbor as yourself.'"

These aren't our words; these are the words of the very man every Christian church claims to follow.

A disease of hate runs deep in our nation's bones; it's permeated our psyche and can be found everywhere. From watercoolers to coffee shops to pulpits to political rallies, hate is often in the driver's seat on both sides of any issue, creating deeper and wider lines of separation. And Jesus' two simple commands are the only things that will remedy this epidemic.

But what does this kind of love look like? If we return to Jesus' teachings in Matthew, we get a pretty clear picture of love as God intended:

> The King will say to those on his right, "Come, you who are blessed by my Father, inherit the kingdom prepared for you from the foundation of the world. For I was hungry and you gave me food, I was thirsty and you gave me drink, I was a stranger and you welcomed me, I was naked and you clothed me, I was sick and you visited me, I was

in prison and you came to me." Then the righteous will answer him, saying, "Lord, when did we see you hungry and feed you, or thirsty and give you drink? And when did we see you a stranger and welcome you, or naked and clothe you? And when did we see you sick or in prison and visit you?" And the King will answer them, "Truly, I say to you, as you did it to one of the least of these my brothers, you did it to me."

MATTHEW 25:34-40, ESV

Feed the hungry.
Welcome the stranger.
Clothe the naked.
Visit the sick and the imprisoned.

When we do these things, not only are we loving those around us, we are actively displaying our love for God.

But so often, we get wrapped up in differing sides and miss the opportunity to love. We spend so much time focused on the "what abouts":

What about the way others have treated me?
What about the "right" or the "left"?
What about the wrongs of past administrations?
What about what he or she said?

These are just distractions from the real problem, distractions that divert our focus from the darkness lurking in our hearts—a darkness that allows us to turn a blind eye to the pain and suffering of others or, worse yet, inflict pain and suffering on others, justifying a doctrine of hate by twisting a gospel of love.

But it doesn't have to be this way—and for many, it's not.

Every day, in every town, in every country, there are people who challenge themselves by asking:

Are my words and actions motivated by love?
Is the life I'm living motivated by love?

Around the globe there are many people doing great things that seem to get lost in the sea of fear and negativity. But still they fight back against the darkness with light. These are people who take Jesus' words and his mission and apply them to every aspect of what they do—and the result is a beauty we all should seek.

Because when we do this, so much more becomes possible. Embracing our call to love as God does is amazing to witness. It's what makes things like shelters for women and children possible. This kind of love takes people to the mission field to meet the needs of the broken; it's what gives each of us the strength to slow down and walk with others in their pain. When churches and organizations lead in this kind of love, with pure motives, the church shines like a city on a hill, a light that no darkness can extinguish.

> **As we build relationships, families, organizations, and communities, we must take care what kind of pieces we put in place. We must use Jesus' teachings as the guide for how, when, and what we build with.**

As we build relationships, families, organizations, and communities, we must take care what kind of pieces we put in place. We must use Jesus' teachings as the guide for how, when, and what we build with. To be a Christian is to follow Christ's teachings, not those of any human. To be a Christian is to use those teachings as the standard for each decision we make, for the actions we choose to support.

When this is our rallying point, the place we run to in life's battles, we live by a standard defined by loving God and loving others—no exceptions.

Broken and Beautiful

16

The world breaks every one and afterward many are strong at the broken places.

– Ernest Hemingway

WE LIVE IN A WORLD obsessed with appearances. Our culture celebrates the unattainable and tries to sell it as things we should have or pursue. Looks, sex, fake body parts, excess in clothes and cars, homes and lifestyle—everywhere we turn, we hear and see messages about how we should be like someone else, that who we are isn't enough. Depression is on a continual rise, the use of anti-anxiety pharmaceuticals is at an all-time high, and each year we turn to new vices, new addictions, new possessions to fill the holes in our hearts and souls.

We don't pretend to have all the answers; in fact, we have very few. But we have come face-to-face with a couple of undeniable truths. The first is that every person is broken in some way, whether it be emotionally, spiritually, or physically. We all have experienced and will continue to experience what it's like to not be whole. And the pain that comes with such struggles—the loss of a loved one, the slow progression of a debilitating disease, trauma, abuse, disability, drug addiction, unemployment, divorce—often becomes a focal point for our lives, voids we try to fill.

However, so much beauty can be found in these hard times. Beauty in the struggle, beauty in the pain, beauty in overcoming each challenge we face. This brings us to the second but more challenging truth—it is only within our brokenness that we can find our true beauty. But to discover this, we can't run from our brokenness. Instead we must embrace it; we must run to it headfirst, arms open, owning all of who we are—but we can't do it alone.

> **It is only within our brokenness that we can find our true beauty.**

———

For more than twenty-five years, I (Justin) have battled a progressive neuromuscular disease. My immune system attacks my motor nerves, and my muscles shut down. I have progressed from using braces to a cane, spent nearly a decade using a manual wheelchair, and now live life from a power wheelchair. I can't feed myself, I have to have someone help me go to the bathroom, and every morning my wife has to dress me. I can't even lift my hand to my face to wipe sweat from my brow or scratch an itch on my leg.

Some people look at me and see a wheelchair; others see a "cripple." Some pity me as someone stricken with disease, while others see me as a burden for those around me. When people look at me, many see someone who is different from them, and sometimes they're not sure what to do with what they see. It's our differences that often make us feel alone. Some are like mine, physical in nature; others rise from life choices or belief systems. But the fact that we are all broken in our different ways can and should be the very thing that unites us.

While I may not be "whole," the hard parts of my life have given me some of my most cherished moments. My brokenness has taken me to places I never knew I could go and has led me into the arms of people I never dreamed of meeting. Life's adventures have taught me many things—they have helped shape my perspective as a friend, spouse, and parent—but it's the people I encounter that teach me the most.

When I first lost the use of my upper body, my wife and I were living in San Diego, California, with our three children. Up to that point I had been a freelance graphic designer, working from home. Each morning I would transfer myself from my bed to my wheelchair, shower, get dressed, enjoy breakfast with my family, and work the rest of the day at my desk. I didn't have my legs, but my hands and mind were strong. But during the winter of 2010, I went from being able to care for myself to being dependent in every way.

> **The fact that we are all broken in our different ways can and should be the very thing that unites us.**

My disease, known as multifocal acquired motor axonopathy (MAMA for short), had plateaued for many years, only affecting me from the waist down, but over the span of six weeks, I lost most of my upper body. Our house was mildly accessible, and we had made it work for my manual wheelchair, but suddenly we needed a new bathroom because I could no longer transfer myself into the shower. We didn't have the money for a remodel and were desperate for help, but we weren't sure where to turn. We didn't have to look far. Friends of ours rallied people from the community. Some were from our church, while others were strangers to us. And with the help of volunteer contractors and vendors donating materials, we had a new accessible bathroom within a few short months.

This was one of the first times I recognized that pain and suffering are often what bring people together; sometimes in the darkness we are at our finest. My home was filled with people who believed differently and lived differently, but they saw my need as a point where they could come together, united by love and compassion. Sometimes it's through our own suffering that we see the beauty with which God made us. Other times, it's through partnering in the pain with others that we get a glimpse of heaven.

Patrick and I have the pleasure of speaking to audiences far and wide. Sometimes we find ourselves in churches, other times in prisons, but most of the time at conferences for businesses and organizations. Regardless of the venue and the clientele, the people we meet all have three things in common—they are in pain, they want the pain to go away, and they're looking for hope.

After each event, we spend time meeting the attendees, listening to their stories, sharing tears as we hear about loss and pain of all kinds. Women who have experienced the worst kind of trauma, parents facing death as disease ravages their bodies, children dying from leukemia, men and women left in wheelchairs much like mine because of accidents, families struggling with unemployment, couples suffering broken marriages, and the list goes on.

With each story, we ask, "How are you doing?" and most of the time we learn of people who have rallied around the individual, guiding them through the pain with patience and grace, setting differences aside because there are more important things than those that divide us. Sometimes it's family, other times a spouse, and still others friends who understand what it means to truly love. We have seen so much beauty rise from the brokenness. The holes that leave so many hearts barely beating are filled with relationships, love, and compassion, and those hearts continue on, fueled by the only thing that will mend our cracks and heal our wounds. We wouldn't wish such painful experiences on anyone, but we have seen firsthand the wonder and beauty God's love brings from them. In the moments where we choose to fill the voids in our brothers and sisters with compassion and mercy, when we choose not to fear the things that make us different from one another and view them as opportunities to unite us, this is where real beauty lies.

But the reality is that for every story of pain countered with people rising up to carry the burden of another, there are stories of shattered lives with no one close by, no one ready to step in or step up—people who are broken but seen as different, people who aren't helped because of past choices, addictions, sexual orientation, or differing beliefs. I can't imagine what my wife and I would have done if a host of people hadn't made a choice to love us in our time of need, regardless of our differences.

Our culture is desperate for a change in focus, a shift from trying to fill our own emptiness with consumption to being the means of filling others' emptiness.

Just a few months ago, Patrick and I met a couple in their late seventies at an event. We struck up a conversation and soon learned they were both on their second marriage. The woman's first husband had died from cancer, and the gentleman's first marriage had ended after he had suffered a stroke causing extreme weakness on his left side.

He told us the story of his first date with his second wife. As they enjoyed dinner, the man said, "I wasn't sure you would want to go on a date with me."

"Why wouldn't I?" the woman asked.

Holding up his limp left arm with his strong and unaffected right hand, he said, "Because I'm not whole."

She reached across the table, took his weak left hand in her own, and said, "This is what makes you whole. Our brokenness is what God uses to bring us together."

———

Our world needs a new generation of men and women ready to embrace one another's pain and suffering. But they need someone to lead the way. As parents and grandparents, aunts and uncles, teachers and mentors, the men and women of today have remarkable power and influence over the shaping of the men and women of tomorrow. The children in our lives are looking to us for direction, and their understanding of how to love and give selflessly will depend on how we love and give.

Our society is filled with messages that scream "be like him" or "dress like her." Through news and politics that propagate fear and dissension, differences have become focal points for conflict and pain rather than something to celebrate. But stepping into conversations about differences with love and grace is one of the most important and formative things we can do for the children we love. So where do we start?

> **The men and women of today have remarkable power and influence over the shaping of the men and women of tomorrow.**

We begin by acknowledging that we are all different and that our differences shouldn't be feared but embraced. We start by recognizing that we are all broken in our own way and that from our brokenness can come so much beauty: beauty in overcoming challenges together, beauty in others doing for us what we can't do on our own, beauty in lifting others up knowing that they will one day do the same for someone else.

In Matthew 25, as Jesus tells the parable of the goats and the sheep, he gives us essential guidelines for how we should live and lead our children—feed the hungry, give drink to the thirsty, invite the stranger in, clothe the naked, care for the sick, visit the imprisoned.

Because we are all hungry and thirsty—hungry for love, thirsty for purpose. We will all be a stranger at some point in time, outcast because of the way we think, live, or believe. We will all be stripped naked by life's circumstances and experience sickness, and we all are or have been prisoners to something—fear, weakness, addictions, a diagnosis. We are all broken in our different ways, but when we come together to carry each other, we are beautiful. The image God created us in—his own—shines brightly when we love as he loves.

> The image God created us in—his own—shines brightly when we love as he loves.

The greatest beauty we can ever experience is only made real through our brokenness.

What do we do to counter the negative impact our culture has on future generations? We embrace our differences through love and teach our children that we are all broken and beautiful.

Every person we meet is broken, and every one of us can be a source of love, grace, mercy, and compassion that makes the broken places the strongest points in their lives. It is only through our brokenness that the power and love of God can be fully known.

Make
Something New

17

Forgiveness says you are given another chance to make a new beginning.

– Desmond Tutu

WHEN THEY WERE YOUNGER, whenever one of our sons or daughters got a new LEGO set for a birthday or Christmas gift, they would immediately put it together, following the instructions so they could replicate the picture on the box—page by page, step by step, piece by piece. The results of their work would sit on a desk or bedside table for a few days, but the real fun came later. On lazy Saturdays, they would dump out a bin filled with different LEGO pieces—a hodgepodge of shapes and colors from who knows how many different sets—and just build, connecting pieces as thoughts and ideas came to their minds. A spaceship here, a fort there. A fairy garden. An all-terrain rover that could handle carpet, hardwood, and the vertical climb up the side of a couch.

There was no limit to what they could build, no rules to follow. They would just create, using the pieces available to make something new.

Whenever we would sit on the floor and build alongside our children, we were reminded of when we used to spend hours doing the same thing as kids. Some of our first memories as friends are of warm summer days when we would spread out a blanket on the grass in the front yard, dump out a bin of miscellaneous LEGO bricks, and go to work. We must have been four or five. There we sat, using whatever pieces were available to make something new.

Any time we hear the word *creativity*, it's easy to think of paintings, drawings, music, or literature. But the word comes from the Latin term *creō*, which simply means to create or make. Not creating a painting, illustrating a drawing, composing music, or writing a book . . . just create or make. While the vast majority of individuals don't find themselves in careers where they create art, write books, or compose music, everyone is capable of so much creativity. However, most of us lose sight of it as we grow older and, as a result, we miss out on a lot of the beauty that exists around us—until we see the world through the eyes of our children.

Several years ago, we heard a talk given on the power of creativity and the wonder of this gift that God has given each person. The speaker stood on the stage at the front of a large church. Off to his side sat a huge pile of LEGOs—tens of thousands of pieces, in every possible shape and color. At the beginning of his talk, the speaker invited all the kids in the crowd to join him on stage and play with the LEGOs.

A host of young boys and girls built as thoughts formed and ideas evolved, and while their imaginations came to life, the man spoke about the creativity that each of us is born with, the image of God we are created in, and the propensity of each man and woman to lose touch with this gift. Periodically, he would pause, approach one of the children on stage, and ask them to tell him about their creations.

The answers included spaceships, trees, a dog, houses, and

race cars. Eventually, some of the boys and girls took apart their work and began making something different; others added onto what they had already built. As time passed, most of the creations changed, evolving into something that previously had not existed.

When the man asked one child what he was doing as the boy added new pieces, the boy said, "I found some new shapes; I want to see what they can make."

The speaker compared the wonder and creativity of a child to our potential as adults to take what life gives us—our experiences, the good and the bad—and make something beautiful. Our moments of love, grace, mercy, and forgiveness combine with our trauma, pain, and regrets to make the pieces of our lives. Sometimes we have to take the pieces apart and rebuild; other times we need to add new pieces to make something better. We can put the pieces together so that only the dark parts show, or we can choose to let others see the beauty of our lives, the light and love shining through the pain.

> **Our moments of love, grace, mercy, and forgiveness combine with our trauma, pain, and regrets to make the pieces of our lives.**

———

In his book *It Was On Fire When I Lay Down On It*, Robert Fulghum tells a story from the Second World War. German paratroopers invaded the island of Crete. When they landed on the shores of the village of Maleme, the islanders met them, armed with nothing but simple farm tools. The outcome was catastrophic. Men, women, and children from the local villages were lined up and shot because of their resistance—entire families wiped out in a few short seconds.

Today, the Maleme airstrip rests below an institute for peace and understanding. This institute was started by a man named Alexander Papaderos. Papaderos was just six years old when World War II started. During the invasion of Crete, his home village was decimated, and he along with many other villagers was imprisoned in a Nazi concentration camp. At the end of the war, Papaderos was filled with a longing for his people to let go of the hatred the war had left in its wake. To help the process, he built his institute where so much pain and destruction had been inflicted on his people.

> "With what I have I can reflect light into the dark places of this world—into the black places in the hearts of men—and change some things in some people."

Years later, Papaderos stood at the front of a lecture taking questions at the close of one of his talks. Fulghum raised his hand and called out, "What is the meaning of life?" The room was filled with nervous laughter and wide eyes—such a weighty question with so many possible answers! Holding up his hand for quiet, Papaderos said, "I will answer your question."

Quietly, Papaderos retrieved his wallet, and removed a piece of glass. Wordlessly, he stared at the small round mirror in his hand. Taking a breath, he raised his eyes from the mirror to the class, and held it up for everyone to see. Then Papaderos answered the question with a story:

When I was a small child, during the war, we were very poor and we lived in a remote village. One day, on the road, I found the broken pieces of a mirror. A German motorcycle had been wrecked in that place.

I tried to find all the pieces and put them together, but it was not possible, so I kept only the largest piece. This one. And by scratching it on a stone I made it round. I began to play with it as a toy and became fascinated by the fact that I could reflect light into dark places where the sun would never shine—in deep holes and crevices and dark closets. It became a game for me to get light into the most inaccessible places I could find.

I kept the little mirror, and as I went about my growing up, I would take it out in idle moments and continue the challenge of the game. As I became a man, I grew to understand that this was not just a child's game but a metaphor for what I might do with my life. I came to understand that I am not the light or the source of light. But light—truth, understanding, knowledge—is there, and it will only shine in many dark places if I reflect it.

I am a fragment of a mirror whose whole design and shape I do not know. Nevertheless, with what I have I can reflect light into the dark places of this world—into the black places in the hearts of men—and change some things in some people. Perhaps others may see and do likewise. This is what I am about. This is the meaning of my life.[2]

Alexander Papaderos could have hated those who persecuted him. He could have let the horrors of war darken his heart. He had watched as his friends and neighbors were murdered in the streets of his hometown, then he was carried away to a concentration camp, where he saw the same things happen again. He had every earthly reason to hate those who turned his world upside down.

But this man's life is summed up in eleven simple words, *I can reflect light into the dark places of this world.*

---

[2] Fulghum, *It Was On Fire When I Lay Down On It*, (New York: Random House, 1988), 174–75.

We don't know what was going through young Papaderos's mind as he took a shattered piece of a mirror and fashioned it into a cherished keepsake, but we do know that he took what was broken and made something new. His creativity as a child helped shape his future. And that homemade toy was the beginning of Alexander Papaderos's path of forgiveness. He was able to take the painful pieces he'd been given and create a life of purpose, a life filled with love. So many of the pieces we need to make a new life rest in forgiveness, grace, mercy, and love—purposeful love, intentional love, love that comes to life through actively loving others.

> So many of the pieces we need to make a new life rest in forgiveness, grace, mercy, and love—purposeful love, intentional love, love that comes to life through actively loving others.

Papaderos understood his purpose. He recognized that the best way he could actively show love to the God he believed in was through loving others.

Living and loving well often means we have to make something new—create a new perspective, find a new understanding, embrace a new paradigm of love as we are drawn deeper into what it means to reflect God's light into the lives of others. Embracing a life worth living means embracing forgiveness and loving as God loves.

This means letting go of our anger and bitterness, pursuing others as God has pursued us—this should be the heartbeat of every human, the heartbeat of every church.

But for this to happen, each of us has to be willing to make a new life, pursue a different understanding of compassion, and live by a new standard of what it means to love God:

Loving God is loving all of his children, not just the ones we want to love.

Loving God is loving those who think differently than we do.

Loving God is loving those who live differently than we do.

Loving God is loving those who worship differently than we do.

Loving God is loving those who believe differently than we do.

Loving God is loving others even if they don't want to be loved.

Within this kind of love is a newness we are invited into; it is the outcome of divine creativity. All the pieces of life we have been given can be put together, reworked, and utilized so that we can make something new with our pieces—a life that loves like Papaderos.

We all are fragments of a mirror whose whole design and shape we do not know. Nevertheless, with what we have we can reflect light into the dark places of this world—into the black places in the hearts of men—and change some things in some people. Perhaps others may see and do likewise. Perhaps others will pick up the pieces they have been given and make something new.

This is what we are about.

This is the meaning of our lives.

Are you ready? Spread out your blanket, dump out the pieces of your life. Pick them up, one by one, examine them, take in all the colors, and ask yourself, "What can I use this for?" Put your pieces together in a new way. Let God's love flow through you as you create a life worth living.

It's never too late to make something new.

Acknowledgments

Collective

So many people go into making a book possible.

A very special thank you to Angela Scheff and Christopher Ferebee for taking us on at your agency and for believing in us. Angela, we can't thank you enough for the guidance and encouragement and all the phone calls that helped us keep going.

To the Tyndale team, you continue to amaze us with your ideas and work ethic. We are blessed to be a part of your team.

Compassion International, thank you for partnering with us on this journey.

MNOP, you are an amazing group of men and women who teach us so much. Thank you for the love you so freely give, the long talks about the things that matter, and so much laughter over good food and good wine. You are our church!

Seth Haines, you are a gifted man. Thank you for sharing your God-given talents with us.

Jim Souza, Jerry McConnell, and Rick Daniels, thank you for sharing your stories and for introducing us to some incredible people who have helped shape who you each have become. Their stories are now a part of ours, and we are better for it.

To those whose names have been changed or who offered stories anonymously, we are grateful for the lessons you have taught us.

This book is about those who leave imprints on others. We both can point to many men who have done so for us. To our boys, friends new and old, we thank you. Brian Snyder, Greg Sanner, and Chris Scott—you made so much of our childhoods worth remembering, love you guys! Michael Turner, Andy Hampton, Tim Bryant, Dave Kluksdal, Brian Martin, Randy Green, Ted Hardy—you are our tribe, thank you for walking in life with us!

From Patrick

My life is filled with people who have walked with me and sometimes for me, and who have carried me when I couldn't find the strength to continue on my own.

Jerry and Karyn Gray, thank you for being my mom and dad. You taught me how to love, instilled in me the beginnings of my faith, and filled my life with so many fond memories. Your love and support have made much of my life possible.

To Jeff Gray and Susan Pennington, I love you guys. Thank you for the laughter and good food over the years. Jeff, I appreciate all the Words with Friends games—you help keep my mind sharp. Killian, I love your humor and wit. Thank you for being an awesome nephew!

Jennifer and Dean Coon, you guys have lifted me through many prayers over the years. Those mean so much. Your love and support is something I will always cherish. James, you are a wonder filled with joy and light. Your smile and laugh warm my heart. I look forward to seeing the man you become.

To Michael and Kathleen Gray, thank you for your constant support over the years. Michael, your friendship has done more for me than you will ever know. Lila and Sophie, you make every room light up; I can't wait to see what you do to the lives you encounter when you grow older.

Kenoyer clan, you are all such beautiful people! I am so glad I get to be a part of your family. Ellen, you are a wonderful woman (and mother-in-law) with such a beautiful heart for others. Doug, Megan, Taylor, Naomi, and Oliver, thank you for being such a wonderful family. Heidi, thank you for all the good times filled with laughter and all things nerdy.

I have been blessed to know several men who are a few steps ahead of me in the journey of life. Howard King, I don't see you often, but when I do, I learn something every time. When I grow up, I want to be like you. Jim Souza, talks of life over beer and good food never get old; thank you for all the wisdom. Ed Castledine, thank you for mentoring me in business, in life, and faith. To all three of you, know you are loved.

Michael Gray, Timothy Bryant, and Trevor Lubiens, thank you for listening to my thoughts and writings over the past year. Your feedback and insights have been formative in the shaping of this book. Whatever happens, I'll go with you.

Jason Touhy, our conversations have meant more to me than I can express in words. Thank you for being there, checking in, and holding me accountable.

Cambria, Joshua, and Olivia—you are such incredible children. Not a day goes by where I don't thank God for you. I have learned more about life and love from being your dad than from anyone else. Thank you for all the lessons found in the daily adventures. You each will leave a lasting impact on all you meet. You inspired the majority of the words in these pages, and each page is what I hope for you in your futures. I love you!

Saving the best for last—Donna, I love you. Thank you for all the hours listening to the words in these pages, for the feedback and insight, and all the nights on the couch—best dates ever! The opportunity to be your husband is the greatest gift I have ever been given. I know there are times I give you reasons to doubt me, but in spite of those reasons, you always choose to have faith in me. Your steadfast love and dedication are the fire that fuels so much of what I do. Thank you for being my wife and my best friend, and for helping me discover the person I am meant to be.

From Justin

Below is a small list of individuals who have deeply impacted me, shaping the person I am today. To you all, I am deeply grateful.

To my parents, Floyd "Jim" and Mavis Skeesuck, you are the two most amazing parents any son could have. You have been by my side through thick and thin and continue to champion my efforts. I love you and thank you for your continued prayers and for dealing with all my sarcasm. (Dad, I think I get it from you, just sayin'.)

To my big brother, Ryan, my sister-in-law Tara, my niece Jillian, and my nephew Zach Skeesuck, thank you for continuing to love me and support me through everything. Ryan, you are an amazing brother, and I appreciate your fatherly insight.

To my little sister, Josie, and my brother-in-law Timel Ragland, I cherish the times we get to spend together, even though they are few and far between. Sis, thanks for being such a wonderful light in the world, not only for me but for all whom you come in contact with.

To the Karlson family: Gary and Maureen (my favorite mother-in-law), Erik and Leticia, Marissa and Paris, and to all my nieces and nephews—your unending love and support for me and my marriage to Kirstin has meant the world. I love you all!

To my mentor, Jim Johnson, over the past twenty-plus years, you have been such a wonderful rock for me. Though we are miles apart, every time I think of you it brings me joy! Thank you for being a wonderful Christ-centered man—a model I strive for every day.

To these men: Patrick Gray, Greg Werner, Brett Wilson, Chad Lansford, Greg Laswell, Mike de Neve, Marcel de Neve, Chris Thirtle, Colin Bowles, Jon Hammer, Scott Peterson, John Parrish, Jamie Gates, Scott Hancock, Ben Powers, Joe Bankard, Mark

Michelson, and my cousin, Todd Taylor. All of you have profoundly impacted me in various ways throughout my life. I cannot thank you enough for the laughter, caring for me through difficult times, accountability for my actions, and making me a better man. Love you guys.

To my three wonderful children, Jaden, Noah, and Lauren, you challenge me every single day to be a better father, and I am grateful for that. All three of you will succeed in life, and I'm hopeful that this book can help guide you in making the world a better place. I am honored to be your father. Thank you for loving me despite all my faults.

Finally, to my amazing wife, Kirstin—words can't express enough how much I love you and how grateful I am to be spending life alongside such a wonderful God-loving woman. I love living life with you, through its ups and downs, and laughing at it—because sometimes you just have to! Thank you for loving me. Thank you for trusting me. Thank you for believing in me. Thank you for having faith in me. I love you, pun-kin.

About the Authors

Patrick Gray and **Justin Skeesuck** have been blessed with a unique friendship that spans more than forty years. Despite the many challenges of a progressive neuromuscular disease robbing Justin of the use of his arms and legs, the two seek to live life without reservations. Their friendship has taken them on many adventures together, most notably their 500-mile wheelchair journey across the vast terrain of northern Spain known as "I'll Push You."

Upon their return from a journey many said was impossible, the two friends began speaking around the globe. As bestselling authors and highly sought-after keynote speakers, Justin and Patrick use their life and work experiences and their adventures as the backdrop against which they explore concepts such as leadership, teamwork, relationships, and the power of human connection.

In 2017 they released their bestselling book, titled *I'll Push You*, a memoir of their friendship and their 500-mile wheelchair journey through Spain. The two friends are also the subjects of an award-winning documentary by the same title.

In April of 2018, they released their children's book, *The Push*, written by Patrick and co-illustrated by Justin.

Patrick lives in Eagle, Idaho, with his wife, Donna, and their three children: Cambria, Joshua, and Olivia.

Justin also lives in Eagle, Idaho, with his wife, Kirstin, and their three children: Jaden, Noah, and Lauren.

To learn more about
Patrick and Justin,
to find out how to
sponsor a child through
Compassion, and to
claim your FREE book
bonuses, please visit
pushinc.us/imprints.

HELPING CHILDREN FALL IN LOVE WITH JESUS SO THEY CAN FALL IN LOVE WITH THE WORLD.

Children all over the world have the same needs: to be known, loved, cared for, and protected.

For some children, having these needs met is a delightful reality. But for many others, it is almost impossible to experience, because extreme poverty tells them they don't matter. Although poverty is often measured materially, it spills out emotionally and spiritually as well.

Jesus had compassion on the poor. When your children love Jesus and see the world through His eyes, compassion is a God-inspired response to need. Tyndale and Compassion International come together to create resources to help children fall in love with Jesus so they can follow His example to love others—especially those who live in poverty.

YOUR LOVE FOR ONE ANOTHER WILL PROVE TO THE WORLD THAT YOU ARE MY DISCIPLES. —JOHN 13:35

Compassion
in Jesus' name
Releasing children from poverty

OUR JOURNEY ON THE CAMINO DE
SANTIAGO TRAIL WAS THE FOCUS OF THE
DOCUMENTARY **I'LL PUSH YOU.**

TO WATCH THE TRAILER AND LEARN
MORE ABOUT THE FILM, PLEASE VISIT:
ILLPUSHYOU.COM

CP1241